SHIFT!

FROM *FEAR* TO FAITH!

Facing Adversity and Winning in Life!

A Personal Journey

SHIFT!
FROM *FEAR* TO FAITH!
Facing Adversity and Winning in Life!
A Personal Journey

DAVINA STALLWORTH
HOPEFULL MESSENGER

SHIFT! FROM FEAR TO FAITH
Facing Adversity and Winning in Life!
A Personal Journey

All scripture quotations, unless otherwise indicated are taken from the New King James Bible Version.

ISBN: 978-0-9994648-3-0

Printed in the United States by Alaska Printing, INC.

Edited By: Cynthia M. Portalatín
creativewords4light@gmail.com

Cover Design: B-EZ-Graphix

What I present to you are my personal life adventures fear, and faith. These passages contain stories of encouragement that are designed to take you from living a life of fear to a powerful, life changing faith. I want to bring you to a place designed by God where you can begin to dream again and rediscover hope. "Shift! From fear to Faith," has been designed to move you out of what is normal to you – that is out of a "fearing mentality" to a place of having a life of success. This place will also be known as your personal, supernatural mindset, by speaking into existence who you are and what you want to become.

In other words, change the way you think, and you WILL change your life. Here in these pages you will find hope, receive a second chance at life and rediscover your dreams. My desire is that you connect with the greatness and beauty that is already in you. You are designed for a purpose. You do have the power within you to move mountains. And "yes," it all starts with how you see yourself. It does not matter what others think of you. What matters is what you think and how you see yourself. You must accept being comfortable in your own skin.

ACKNOWLEDGEMENTS

All honor and glory to Jesus Christ. It is because of Him I can declare I am able to live a life free from fear, rejection and hopelessness.

A big heartfelt thanks to my wonderful, husband, Michael, and my biggest supporter, who has stood by me through the ups and down! I love you Babe! Mom, thank you for living for Christ and being a Godly example to so many and for your enduring strength. I love you!

To my children, Kevina, Christina, Anna and Michael III and grandkids, I pray to leave a legacy of love and hope to spur you on to live your dreams and live out loud for Christ.

To Pastor Ken and Dr. Deb Friendly, my first Spiritual parents, who taught me about living by Faith! You are a true inspiration in my life without you all and the Lighthouse Christian Fellowship family, I could not write this journey of my life. Thank you for your love and support.

Thank you to Pastor Tommy and Pastor LaTonyea Leonard and New Season Christian Center! Thank you for your love, teachings and living a lifestyle of faith. I am honored to serve with you in the building of the Kingdom of God.

To my Spiritual Dad and Mom, Prophets James and Ruth, you live a life of pure and genuine faith. You have given so much so that Christ will be known throughout the entire earth. You have pushed me, pulled me and stretched me beyond human comprehension. You have lifted me up when I was so low, I was under the ground! But more than anything, you love me unconditionally. Te Amo Familia!

There are so many others to acknowledge, my Dad, Sisters Shawn and Anje, my brother Vince, Aunts, Uncles, cousins and friends. You all are my family and have made my life journey possible. Thank you.

FOREWORD

I have known Davina Stallworth for years and have watched as God rewarded her faithfulness to His word and ministry. Shift!! Is a powerful example of a journey of overcoming the grips of fear and moving into full faith!! If you are ready to make some serious strides toward your purpose and destiny, there can be no better road map than this to your breakthrough.

She masterfully writes in a way that helps readers open their hearts to God and sense the vital importance of living a life of faith and pushing toward God's purpose, free from the incapacitating spirit of fear.

Unfortunately, we won't go through life without opportunities of being intimidated to move forward. Experience tells us that there are moments things don't work out for us as planned. However, we can be free from the fear of failure, because God gives us the ability to redefine our moments. And this book will help you do that! No longer will we be afraid of failing, because in Christ it's just feedback.

This is an important book, a Kingdom treasure! I can't wait to get my copy, and you must have one too!!!

New Season Christian Center
Pastor Tommy Leonard, III, D.D.

TABLE OF CONTENTS

TABLE OF CONTENTS

1

SHIFT! FROM FEAR TO FAITH

The energy in the air was super charged with power as the musicians began to saturate the atmosphere with the sounds of heaven. They played lively melodies which invited heaven into the room! The music doused every present soul with expectation! The house was full of people from all over the city who had come not to see a show but to experience heaven and hear the teaching of the powerful, life-changing Word of God.

It was an energizing service cloaked in the presence of God! Who would not want to be in such a dynamic place? Sweat poured from every pore of her body. Her stomach rolled and settled in knots, and her hands, danced sporadically to an unheard song – clenching then unclenching. Her palms were clammy with sweat. She forbid herself from wiping her hands on her new white garments.

Noticeably trembling, her knees knocked with fear as she imagined every possible scenario of danger, disaster and dim wittedness: tripping over her feet, or her shirt flying up in her face, and let's not forget her favorite – forgetting the choreography! Oh! What the mind can conceive in the event of possible peril (all imagined of course).

Her tongue was stuck to the roof of her mouth, because it seemed the Sahara Desert had taken a vacation within it! Wasn't it hotter than usual in the sanctuary? What about spacing? There was no way they would be able to dance out there; the front row was practically on the platform! But she knew there was plenty of space. Her mind seemed to be playing tricks on her! Her eyes darted back and forth across the room, searching for a quick way of escape, just in case she flipped over a chair on the way to the front of the church. The only way to depart the premises was to run swiftly past the throngs of people who were crowded into the main sanctuary and would be watching what was to come.

"How she could do such a thing?" she thought feverishly.

What was she thinking?! Just because someone says, "we want you to be the dance team leader," doesn't mean you are supposed to jump up and do it! Well, it was a little too late for second thoughts now.

Dancing was her source of enjoyment. It meant freedom from all things that caused her to shake in her boots. It was her private world, a world without shame or thought, rejection or fear. To let her body do what it was meant to do, was liberality beyond belief. Oh! To dance, dance, dance!

As a small child, she was awkward, clumsy and had no rhythm. But one day, she awakened to the sound of beautiful music playing in her ear. At that moment, she understood the rhythm of the song! The sound drifted between her ears and into her heart, awakening something so hidden, she didn't even know it existed.

2

This sound, this movement, was the catalyst that was a part of changing her life! In it she heard an unspoken language.

This soulful sound also awakened her heart and soul to the magic of the invisible colors and hues of a hidden world! In this world, she was accepted. She was majestic and could move as the wind if she so desired. As her body swayed to the music, it began to make sense to her, and her body heard the cadence of the rhythm in the music and responded to the sound like a leaf tossed in a summer breeze in a long-forgotten meadow.

Dancing made her believe she was special. Dancing calmed her, and she became a beautiful Princess. The world was a beautiful and forgiving place when she listened to the welcoming sound waves of music. She and a litany of dancers moved majestically to the music, telling the story of the song in her head and of what the music spoke to her spirit.

A few months prior, she was asked to form and lead a dance team at her church.

"Okay, I'll do it," she said without even thinking.

It seemed a strange request, but the plan of heaven could not be stopped, no matter how petrified she was. After the phone call, she was shocked, but pressed ahead. No one had ever asked her to do such a great thing like this! However, Corina, the church music director, was someone she admired, respected and trusted. So of course, she knew what she was talking about in asking her.

Well, here she was with the Praise dance team! Success or failure – this was the moment. She'd prayed, fasted, rehearsed, and believed. Now with fear attacking her every thought, wanting to run away, she stood her ground and waited. Her nerves were a wreck; her heart beat furiously through the thin wall of her chest, and her knees knocked till she could hardly stand. But she took the walk to the front of the church with the rest of the team.

3

The celebration of praise in the dance began, and the entire house joined in adoration and celebration of the King.

We leapt, jumped and spun! It was a glorious beginning! This was the start of my first acceptance of God's assignment in my life, and it began with the much, needed deliverance from fear.

This is my story, my personal journey from fear to living a life of faith. I decided to turn over a new leaf, because I'd been living the same story year after year, day in and day out. I didn't know how to breathe, but I knew there was a way to do it – that is to live a life of freedom and not just live unafraid. It was time for a new chapter in my life.

Fear had become my closest friend and confidante since childhood. Quiet, sweet and persuasive messages of self-hatred dripped from its lips and flowed into my mind. Its fragrance, a mix of lies and deception, crept into my soul and, with its tendrils of hatefulness, wrapped its putridness around my heart. I ate with fear, conversed with it and lived with it. Fear became my identity, my master, and I belonged to it.

Fear of being alone, fear of death, fear of rejection, fear of pain, fear of drowning, fear of water, fear of darkness - haunted me. I slept with the lights on at night.

Fear had taken away my true self and twisted my heart with evil. I couldn't even stand to look at myself in the mirror. To tell the truth, my mind had become a caged bird wanting to escape an unwanted, torturous hell, the life of living in fear.

All my life I'd adjusted to whatever was thrown at me. My coping mechanism was to read voraciously. I read everything and anything I could get my hands on to escape reality. All through school, I would be so happy to be able to go to the library and read. Reading became my "super power." It allowed me to be free and see inside someone else's life. I also became a part of the stories I read. I was the superhero, the damsel in distress, the adventurer or even the detective. I didn't have to be me anymore. I was anyone I wanted to be, good or bad.

I lived a lonely existence, or so I thought, until I discovered the power of a great imagination! And that power was awakened through living an adventurous life in reading. Reading was my favorite pastime; it was a way for me to escape the present. It also opened my mind to greater possibilities. But the strangest thing was the books I read! Horror novels by the great master of horror himself, Stephen King! I also read thrillers and tales of terror by Dean Koontz and many others. These stories of the paranormal, monsters and the like fed the growing creature in the core of my soul. This was my way of escape and my way of identifying with the world.

People were with me, but I really did not know how to talk to them, because fear hindered me from sharing too many ideas. Believing I would be laughed at and ridiculed, I kept my mouth shut. I did not truly invite anyone in. I was afraid they would leave me or hurt me. So, my defense mechanism was to build up a wall. A wall so high, I could not get out nor could anyone come in.

I remember a time when I began to recognize the power of fear. When I was a little girl, my Mother enrolled my sister, brother and I in swimming classes. One particular, hot summer day, the sun mercilessly beat down upon the backs of the swimmers, and the swim coach wanted us to dive off the diving board into the cool, crystal clear pool. It was so inviting! The coolness of the water, swam in the thoughts of the children's minds.

What a pleasant, refreshing and desirable invitation the water appeared to be! To most it was a breathtaking plunge into heaven itself. However, to me it spoke of suffering to breathe, sinking into oblivion and even death.

A few years earlier, I'd fallen into the very same pool and nearly drowned. I had accidently fallen into the deep end of the pool. As a tiny and insecure child of five or six-years-old, I decided right then and there, subconsciously of course, I was done with water! Okay, showers and baths were still in, because there was no way my Mom would let me go anywhere without being spotlessly clean! Otherwise, water and I had an understanding – we could no longer be friends!

When my turn came to jump, I sat on the end of the diving board and shook uncontrollably. Truthfully, I wanted to dive into the water, but so many scenarios ran through my head, I couldn't move past that moment of drowning. No one could move me! I was scared, and I was crying. There was no way I was jumping into the jaws of death! I didn't care how pretty the water looked. I could go home and get in the tub!

The sun beat down upon my skin, and it seemed to cook my flesh. I didn't care… if I was burned to a crisp, then so be it! I was completely and utterly terrified!

All the other kids were ready to jump in to cool their burning skin from the incessant heat as the sun seemed to climb higher by the minute. Eventually, after threats of being thrown off the diving board, I appeased the angry mob by removing myself from the scene. I skedaddled back down the ladder from which I'd come, while the eyes of those who'd been angrily waiting, in the boiling hot sun, stared at me with pure hatred. The only thing I cared about was departing the premises!

Fear kept me from jumping off that diving board. I was even afraid to put my head under the water when I took a shower, because I thought I was going to drown! Drowning while standing up in a shower, now that's something! My heart would beat so fast, and I couldn't breathe! Fear, my faithful companion had his talons in me and refused to let me go!

But worse than the stories were people. I wanted to please people, because I wanted to be a part of their lives. Unfortunately, I also was terrified of making someone angry. As a youngster, I would try to fit in to become like someone else. As I grew older, I came to the realization that I didn't know who I was. I did not even know I had an identity! Survival was my only mindset.

As I sit here and reason, I can only come to one conclusion: my God-given identity had been stolen by the spirit of fear. This spirit had me wrapped in a cocoon so tight, it was as if a giant python was squeezing the life out of me. Confrontation was a total "no way, we do not go down that street ever!" I was trapped in my own world of pleasing people at almost any cost.

People would treat me poorly, talk about me in a negative manner, in my face and behind my back, and they were supposed to be my friends. They would make fun of me or use me as a door mat. I knew it was wrong, but I wanted to be liked and accepted. How could I be, when I did not even know who I was?

The thoughts in my head ran rampant!

"You are nobody!"

"No one likes you!"

"You are too dumb for anyone to get to know you!"

"Nobody wants to be around you!"

I tried to anticipate the actions of the people who were my "friends," but I was a victim of their actions. I was afraid to admit I was being treated unjustly. I just wanted to be liked, accepted and even loved. To combat against being hurt, I became very cold hearted and mean. This was my armor, my self-defense. I became like they were. I looked for others who I assumed were weaker than I. It made me feel stronger and empowered.

Once, in middle school, I wanted to befriend a young girl who was about my age. I decided to pick a fight with her because people rejected me, and I wanted to reject someone else. We started with mean words, which elevated to a kicking match and in turn a fight. We were stopped by our teachers, but I've remembered why I fought her even to this day.

My tongue became my weapon. It could be as sweet to you as honey or sharp as a knife and cut you to pieces. At this point in my life, as a young adult, it didn't matter whether you liked me or not. I had found my identity in bitterness and hate.

You see, no one knew of this seething demon that wrapped its putrid tendrils around my beating heart. It had become cold and hard – I wanted to bring pain to those who hurt me.

However, here is the very interesting part: I always sought the better, the kindness in people. I believed there was good in people. Therefore, I wanted to do what was right to help others. But I held back because I was scared.

You may ask, "How is this possible?"

This is the constant battle that raged inside of me. I truly loved helping people, and I wanted to bring a

smile to their faces. Compassion was the force that drove me to seek true friendships. Yet, I have met some of the most wonderful people on the face of this earth, and I did not believe I could help them or be a genuine friend, because I needed help myself. I had to be set free.

2

FEAR...CAUSES YOU TO MISS OUT

There were many things that frightened me. I was a high functioning, fear induced person, (if that is really such a thing). There were so many opportunities I missed, because I was scared to try – meeting new people, going places and enjoying new opportunities. For instance, I have a penchant for beautiful clothing from the era of 1920 to the 1950's, and as a clothing designer the magnificent details of these fashion eras cause me to envision my own line of designer clothing someday. Once, many years ago, I met a lady who offered to sponsor me for a full fashion show.

"How are you going to find anyone to sew your stuff? Was I really good enough?"

"Will they like it? Will the garments be acceptable? What if they don't think lit it?"

"What if they don't like me?"

On and on, these thoughts went around in my head. Eventually, fear talked me out of doing the job. As I recalled the missed opportunity, I can say I regretted not taking her up on the offer. I used to wonder what would have happened if I'd stuck with it.

Today, I can say there are no regrets. But at that time, it was very difficult for me to believe anyone would even consider trusting me to do anything significant. Because when I looked in the mirror, I saw a failure.

Who was I? I didn't believe in myself, nor did I believe I could accomplish anything great. In my state of "fear," I couldn't see beyond what was in front of me. My entire life was based on survival, this was my day-to-day busy. Pretending was my game – that is to be something I was not. I was a chameleon with no real colors, no true identity.

Whenever I was asked, "who are you?" or "what are your likes and dislikes?" there was no answer I could provide. I drew a complete blank. I was trying not to be me. Eventually, my whole identity shattered into a million pieces like a broken mirror. I had no substance to stand on. For me it was just simply waking up one day, and asking… Who was I? Who had I become? Who was this person staring back at me from the reflection in the mirror?

There are many examples of how I allowed myself to be held back from greatness and from living a joyous life, because I'd let my best friend, "fear" – also known as fear of rejection, intimidation, and timidity – hold me back from becoming the person I truly wanted to be.

Maybe, right now at this moment, you are asking, "how did you crawl out of this hole of fear and despair?" First, I had to accept that I was valuable, and I was destined for greater things than just being a victim. Looking beyond myself and seeing the big picture, I had to recognize that there was someone bigger than I, who held my past, present and future. I had to come to the understanding that my life did not revolve around whether or not people liked me. This realization was a big step towards letting go of fear.

Before I can move forward with telling you how I found my courage, I have to go back to many years ago, when I was a little girl.

I was born in a little town in Georgia, in the 60's. I grew up in the city of Atlanta. I was a quiet child, who pretty much kept to myself. I'd even go so far as to say I was an introvert, who escaped life through the magic of reading, as I mentioned earlier. When reading, I could be anywhere, any place and at any time. I'd hide in stories to escaping the reality and harshness of the cruel world. I loved to read. Reading was my life!

As a child, I was teased mercilessly every day and made fun of because of my face. When I was a little baby, I suffered what may have been a stroke. No one knew what happened, but the left side of my face became paralyzed. So, when I smiled, the right side of my face moved fine, but the other side of my face was motionless, with no muscle movement at all.

I went from being a beautiful picture doll of a baby to an ugly, useless and broken china doll. No one knew how or what happened. My Mom came home from work one day, and the babysitter who had been watching me could not give an explanation as to what happened to me. No one had any answers. Doctors could not present a cure nor treat what they did not know. This one event changed the course of my life.

I grew up believing I was ugly. When I looked in the mirror, I saw a face that was lopsided. I saw a shyness, shame and sorrow. I saw me. I became what I'd heard: UGLY. Believing I was deformed, not worthy of anything or anyone. Beauty was not a part of my life; that was not me. Pretty, attractive or cute were not words I was used to hearing. It didn't matter if someone said it, I did not listen because of what I believed about myself. I did not believe them; I believed the truth as I saw it. My lips were crooked. I could not fully close my eyes, nor could I blink fully with my left eye. Smiling was a complete disaster! I had an overbite and spaces throughout my top row of teeth. When I laughed, I always covered my mouth with my hands; so, no one could see how my face twisted.

I cried a lot of tears of self-hate, bitterness and pain. I didn't want to be ugly. Grasping why I was on this earth could not register in my mind. I wanted to be beautiful like my oldest sister. Believing I was a nobody, deformed and void of an existence, I allowed my heart to shut down, and I became the essence of darkness and self-hatred. The pain of being repeatedly rejected by people who I respected added to the freight train of baggage I already carried and eventually wreaked havoc on my soul.

There were those who were sent to protect me and keep me out of harm's way as much as possible, but they could not always save me from predators, those who intended to do me harm no matter what. However, God sent an angel to watch over me: my oldest sister Shawn, my hero. She looked out for me at all costs. She was a sophisticated and a classy young lady, however, if you messed with her family, she would beat you to a pulp with the makeup and the heels on. She wouldn't even break a nail! She was one tough young lady!

When I was in the eighth grade, we attended John F. Kennedy middle school together. Of course, even at this new school, I was teased. There was an upper classman who was determined to literally bite my head off. She did not like my sister, and she was set on getting revenge by hurting me in any way possible. This young lady, I'll call her Leslie, would push me and threaten me with a beating whenever she saw me. She would go out of her way to make it known that she did not like me or my sister.

One day, I was walking down the hall with a hall pass, and lo and behold here came Leslie, looking mean as a snake and ready to bite with a vengeance. She pushed me against the wall and began to hit me. Suddenly, it seemed as if the air was sucked out of the hallway. Leslies head reared back, and she had this complete look of terror on her face!

What she didn't know was that at the exact same moment she was getting ready to pummel me to death, my sister walked down the hallway. She grabbed Leslie by her hair and looked at me.

"I will take care of her. You go back to class." she said.

Joy coursed through my body as I leapt. and I turned around as quickly as I could and speedily walked to class.

"THUMP, THUMP, THUMP" was heard behind me as my sister smashed the girl's head against the window.

I did laugh! I laughed so hard my stomach hurt. Finally, I won. My sister told me later that Leslie would never bother me again. And true to her word, that girl never bothered me again.

I felt the love of God smile down on me, and I felt so special and happy. Even though this feeling was short lived, I wanted to feel this way forever. In the years since, I have remembered my Sister as my hero, causing me to believe that somehow, maybe I was worth something.

Maybe there was something out there bigger than I was that had a plan for me. Years would go by before I would know or even consider that God had a plan for my life. It would take an awareness that He existed, and I would have to walk by faith to get to where I needed to be.

3

JOURNEY TO FAITH

My journey to faith was a precarious one – filled with ups and downs, hills and valleys. It was quite interesting. Even though I'd made poor decisions and had gone through many bad spells as a young adult, I would always find my way back to church. The reason why is because of my Mother, her love and her prayers. Everyone called her Ms. Anne. She made sure we went to church every Sunday. She taught me the importance of going to church, and this has been with me throughout my entire life. She would go without just so we could have food to eat and clothes on our back. Now I understand that she was teaching me the importance of having a relationship with the Lord. No matter what happens in life, turn to God.

As I look back on my life, I don't think anyone knew how afraid I was. I kept my secret hidden. I placed the fear in a treasure box and gave it a very special place in my heart.

As a young adult, at the age of 23, I turned back to God, after a time of doing things my own way, and joined a local, small church in Phoenix. I was on the praise and worship team where I could sing as much as I wanted. I truly enjoyed singing gospels songs. I loved God and wanted to bring joy to His heart. He accepted me for who I was, and He truly was my friend.

It was at this place I found my Lord and Savior, and in this same place I let Him go.

I'd made friends at this lovely church. I'd found a people who did not care about how I looked. In the time I was there, my heart began to change. Believing I was accepted as a person, I began to love myself. In time, I set my sight on a handsome gentleman. Let's call him "James." He was kind hearted, compassionate and thoughtful. These qualities I saw began to cause me to wonder if he would want to be with someone like me. Hoping he felt the same way about me, I asked him if I could speak to him alone. Spilling my heart and guts all over the floor, I bashfully declared my feelings for him. He kindly and gently explained his heart was for another.

My heart was broken once again, and at this stage in my life, I did not make friends easily. The Lord knew I didn't need to be in ANY kind of relationship! Healing and deliverance is what I needed. Because of this imagined heartbreak, I left the church. I was too embarrassed to face him ever again. Once again, I began to wander aimlessly through life.

I had no vision, no purpose and no dreams. I existed for the sake of living: work, play, more work, and sleep.

Do you want to hear something funny? Even though I continued to make terrible mistakes, hang around the wrong people, go out to clubs and party, I didn't think about fear – I gave him some much needed rest. Only when I came in touch with the fragility of my humanity, did I remember my old friend was still waiting in the wings.

The bright morning sun touched my sleepy eyes, and the peaceful morning triggered memories from long ago, which caused me to remember my past – the rejection, the abuse and the pain. Fear raised his head, stretched and greeted me with a crooked smile. Again, he was with me like a good cup of coffee in the morning, except he was not good or even tasteful. He constantly reminded me of my past failures, how no one needed me, how that I was "nothing" and "nobody" and would remain that way.

These thoughts caused me to consistently make poor choices such as bad friendships. Boy was I good at that! I did what I did to forget about the pain and the hurt I'd endured. Consciously and subconsciously choosing not to acknowledge my past nor confront it did not negate its existence. It eventually caught up with me. It would take a miracle of faith to get me off this never-ending roller coaster ride.

FAITH...

"Now Faith Is the substance of things hoped for the evidence of things not seen."
Hebrews 11:1

4

WHAT IS FEAR? WHAT IS FAITH?

You may ask, how do I get from fear to faith? What is that going to look like? Is it possible to defeat fear? Is this for any kind of fear? You may even ask, what is Faith? And what does that look like?

What is Fear? It is the absolute absence of faith. It is the belief that if anything could go wrong, it will go wrong. Fear is the plaguing, nagging thoughts that mill around in your head of the worst of the worst, nightmares, night terrors, things that are imagined and sometimes real.

Another word for fear is Phobia: the fear of persons, places or things living or dead; it is the absolute terror of something or someone for instance, people, dogs or clowns.

Fear of change – the inability to adjust or adapt or accept something new and or different; not knowing nor understanding what can happen in the midst of change. Fear of change can be fear of success, fear of animals, fear of public speaking... the list of phobia-causing fears goes on and on.

Have you ever had to give a speech in front of anyone? Or how about leading a song in front of a crowd of 10, 20 or a thousand? Are you afraid of people? Heights? Spiders? Fear has been designed by the enemy to cause you to live a life beneath you.

God says in His word that He has come to give you life and give life more abundantly (John 10:10)! That means a life of joy, prosperity, laughter, strength, and happiness. The enemy, on the other hand, also known as Satan, comes to steal, kill and destroy by breaking your will down, isolating you from family, friends, and by telling you it's better to be alone. His job is to destroy your identity and to eventually destroy you.

5

CHANGING YOUR MINDSET

Change your mindset from fear to faith to victory, and you will encounter a more rewarding life. A person locked in a world of fear will never experience the true beauty of dynamic living. If you choose to stay in fear, the glass you look out of will always be half full which will prevent you from seeing who YOU really are and what you are capable of doing. It will take work to change your mindset, but you can begin by changing your thinking from negative thinking to positive! A person will eventually become what he or she thinks.

Changing your mindset starts with changing your focus. What are you focused on? What are you looking at with your natural eyes? And your mind's eye? Use your God-given imagination to refocus, and see situations and circumstances differently. See things in a better state or even in a more uplifting manner. Begin to see a brighter and more influential future. You have it in you, and all you have to do is BELIEVE! Change your mind set by changing what you focus on. Refocus on living a successful life. What does that look like to you? Are you happy? What does that feel like to you?

Dr. Mike Davis, an emotional and life coach, taught me to live a successful life by living from joy. Envision that circumstance, that storm being annihilated, and see a better outcome. If you don't like being rejected by people, see yourself accepted for who you are. Speak life to yourself as you stare back at yourself in the mirror, and believe better is possible.

6

FROM THE POINT OF FEAR TO THE POINT OF FAITH

As a young child and as a young adult, I was afraid of many things seen, unseen, real, and imagined. One fear I had to overcome was confrontation. Trapped in a world of "people pleasing," I had entered into a cycle of self-destruction to hide my true identity. In order to fit in, I became what I needed to be to win the friendship of others.

Regardless of what I did, people still talked about me in a negative manner. They made fun of my face, or better yet, completely ignored me when I came around. Yet, I still longed for their friendship. As a coping mechanism, I watched people and made up stories about them. This became my way of functioning to cope with people. Believing the best about people is what I chose to do. However, I became a victim to the people I called my friends. It didn't matter how they treated me or talked down to me, I just wanted to be accepted, to be loved.

You see, I was afraid to acknowledge the fear in my heart, because acknowledging the problem before me meant I could lose this friendship I'd gained. Fear of rejection and not wanting to go through the physical pain it caused, caused me to overlook the name calling, disrespect and disparaging jokes. This was a horrible way to live in any way or on any day of the week! This was another layer of the onion added to the many layers of fear that were already present.

Fear had become the stronghold that gripped the very core of my life. Like a parasite, I permitted it to suck the life out of me. It robbed me of a productive lifestyle. You may ask, how did this start? How could this happen? There is not just one incident, but being in school and suffering from a low self-esteem were a big part of the problem.

7

SCHOOL OF LITERAL
HARD KNOCKS

As a child, I welcomed school. I believed it to be a place where a child could grow, learn and have lifelong friends. My school life was filled with bullying, hate and much pain. Initially, I came to school as a little girl with an open heart and with hope that maybe I could have a true friend. I was scared on that first day of elementary school, and unfortunately it set the precedence for years to come.

I looked forward to new friends and even possible acceptance. However, that door was quickly slammed in my face, because it seemed I was different from everyone else. School became my personal hell. Kids called me, "Ugly, Stupid and Dumb." They would pull my hair, push me down onto the ground, and would pick at me mercilessly.

Tears were constantly in my eyes. I was called names

such as "crip-lip," "crooked lips" and a host of other terrible names. I was embarrassed and extremely sad. I hated going to school. The worst part was being totally ignored. It was as if I was never born.

My face became a source of fear to others, because it was not like their faces. I kept thinking and believing I would not be accepted, because I was not considered normal or in this case pretty. Kids can be, and were, very cruel. They seemed to lack reasoning behind what they did, only desiring to satisfy their need to produce a chain reaction of destruction at my expense.

They punched me with their fists, kicked me, and rejected everything about me. The kids hated me, because they looked upon me as something not worthy of a kind word nor friendship – at least this is how I felt.

Lacking self-confidence didn't help either. I was very quiet and withdrawn. I had no desire to bring attention to myself. The actions of the kids, hitting and calling me names, only succeeded in sealing the belief that I was unworthy of friendship and not worth loving. The side effect of this treatment only caused the darkness within to grow stronger.

Believing I did not matter, I became a nobody. On the playground, I was always the last one chosen or not picked at all for games during recess. There were teachers, like Ms. Davis and Ms. Jackson, who came to my rescue and tried to "save," me. They pointed out my good qualities and told me I was kind, smart and thoughtful, but to no avail – I was still me, wrapped up in a shell of rejection and fear. It did not matter what they said or did, I was still me.

You know you have it bad when the kid no one likes picks on you. Once, on my walk home from school, this kid who was an obnoxious pest began to call me names real loud. My oldest sister and little brother were with me. I warned him to leave me alone, but he wouldn't listen. I'd had a bad day and was fed up by the whole "bullying" scenario. So, I started screaming, yelling and crying at the top of my lungs, and I took off running after him like a complete crazy person! His eyes practically bulged from their sockets; he was so terrified! I know I scared his socks off! He screamed and took off running like a shot! He was totally not expecting this kind of reaction. With all my might, I took off after him! Running at top speed, time had no meaning and seemed to slow down as I gained upon my target. I almost caught him! He jumped over a short brick wall and kept on running! I did not go after him, although I wanted to. As I look back on that day, I know if I'd caught him, I would have beat the snot out of him!

There was another occasion where one of my classmates, J., asked to look at a birthstone ring my mother had bought me for my birthday. I let her see it, and she said she would give it back after lunch. Later in the day I asked for my ring back, and she said she dropped it outside. I was furious, but scared. My Mom was going to kill me for losing that ring! I ran outside and looked for that ring. I never found it, of course. Later I found out she had it and would not give it back. I didn't even think a person would do that. I cried, because my mother gave me that ring and it was very special to me.

Another time in class, Robert (not his real name) began to poke me in my back. My desk was right in front of his, and he called me bad names under his breath. I could hear everything he said, and it hurt to hear his words. He continued to do this as his fingers poked harder and harder. Angrily, I turned around to face him and told him to stop picking at me. Suddenly, his fist connected with my face! Whoa! Where did that come from? My head rocked from side to side as blood spurted from my nose and mouth. Feeling as if the world was against me, without thinking, I turned towards my desk, picked up a huge, hard backed reading textbook and hit him across the face with it.

SMACK! The sound that emitted from the book as it came in contact with the face of my tormentor was thunderous! There was not a sound to be heard in the classroom. Time seemed to suddenly stop. No one breathed. I can't tell you what everyone else did. At this point, he must have passed out, because I did not hear a peep out of this guy after that!

Immediately I sat down at my desk and bawled like a baby. My face hurt, but not worse than my feelings. I could hear the teacher yelling at me to get out of her classroom and go to the Principal's office. But not once did I hear her tell the boy who hit me to get out. With my face on my desk and my arms wrapped around my head to hide from the shame of being bullied once again, I got up with no assistance from my teacher. Tears and snot mixed with the blood that ran from my nose and mouth. I and a classmate left the classroom and headed to the principal's office. All I could think of was my teacher did nothing to protect me. She did nothing to help me; she did not even stop the boy from hurting me.

My sister met me in the principal's office that day. She was very upset. I honestly do not remember what happened afterwards. I do know I eventually forgave this teacher, but I had to in order for the healing of my heart to begin.

It seemed I fought my way through, or mostly got beat up at, school. My sister and brother fought for me when they could, but they could not be with me all the time. To escape, I daydreamed… I did a lot of dreaming. I dreamed to change who I was. I dreamed of being a princess, being whisked away on a white horse to a place of freedom. Free to dance! To Play! And just be Me. Those were my dreams, and they kept me going for a little while.

As I grew older, I learned dreams die. Fear was in my heart and in my head. Fear caused me to believe that no matter what I did I could never do anything right. Even the way I saw myself as not pretty, cute or attractive had its roots in this fear. I avoided looking in mirrors as much as possible. When I did look in the mirror, I focused on what I had to do, so I would not see what I'd become.

Eventually, as I grew older, a new identity began to emerge, and I began to copy what I saw others do. I became a follower. Quickly, I learned what worked for others just might work for me too!

If you don't know who you are, you will become anything that is put in front of you – like tofu, a type of soybean product that takes on the flavor of whatever you put next to it. It's like a parasite, it sucks the flavor out of foods it is placed next to.

I would watch people, just to see how they acted in situations, how they walked and talked. Observing others became my "time-passer." Even though I watched people, I don't even think I was aware I watched so intently. Looking at people and observing their ways, I would imagine their lives were picture perfect, and I wanted to be that way too. So, I tried to become what I saw.

If someone was wearing an outfit that I liked, I would search for and find a similar outfit. You may think that's okay; no problem, everyone does that, right? This may be true, in some cases, but I had no identity. I was on a journey to literally find out how I fit in this thing called life. I was looking for peace within myself. I did not want to be the person I already was. To me, I was a total loser.

As I observed others, I was unaware of what I was really doing. It did not cross my mind. I would even go so far to say I was subconsciously doing these things. My basic thought was about what I liked or disliked. I had no visions, no dreams and no goals. It did not matter how I fit into this world. My only thought was to live day-by-day. Surviving day-by-day was my lifeline. All my dreams had died long ago as a child.

I loved my older sister; she was absolutely beautiful, strong and captivating! The truth is I wanted to be just like her. She was my Hero! Everything she did was golden! She was the coolest girl in school! Athletes, teachers, punk rockers, thugs, and cheerleaders liked her and wanted to be her friends.

However, there were those who hated her and tried

to hurt her by trying to damage her character, her reputation and even her beauty. There was one incident, when some girls put cherry bombs in her school locker, because they really disliked her. Only by God's grace did they not go off while she was at her locker.

She could fight and put anyone under the table, and she would win every time!

There was no one like my Big Sister Shawn. She was my protector and kept some of the "uglies" away from me as much as possible. Sadly enough, she couldn't be around all the time. I had to learn how to accept myself just as I was. This meant I had to learn to love myself just the way I was – my face, shortcomings and all.

So, when someone suggested or said something that interested me, I adjusted or adapted to make the necessary changes to become the image of that person's interest. The power of agreement was significant to me, even though I did not know what it was. It didn't matter if someone said that the brown cow was really blue. I agreed with that statement. Agreement was easy for me, because I knew if I went along with the conversation, I could possibly "fit in," or get accepted.

The reality of the situation was I was never born to fit in. I was created for a greater purpose. I had yet to figure that out. Until I accepted the "truth," not just a fact, that I was created for something better than just "existing," my world would not change. It was not until many years later that I would discover this truth. At this time, in this season, the upper hand was not in my favor, because this is what I believed…

Gullible and naïve is what I was. In reality, "Naivety," was my middle name. People would "talk" over my head, but what they didn't know was I understood what they were saying. There was not too much they could say, because it had all been said before in my head and by others. Talking down to myself is what I did best. Choosing to ignore the snide comments worked for a little while, but you know, I got tired of it. People eventually caught on that I was not stupid, and they just stopped talking to me altogether.

Keeping myself in mediocrity, just being plain average or below average, was my way of not thinking beyond the moment – to not stand out was my trick of the trade. Preferring to stay in the background was how I wanted to stay.

Predators, people who can sense your weaknesses and shortcomings, can smell you coming a mile away. It seems, those who are being hunted carry a distinct smell, and I am so sure I carried this fragrance of "victim," that I could be identified for miles around. (I could have marketed this scent and become a millionaire, if I had not been so scared to sell it!)

At the age of 18, I left home and joined the military. I'd gotten the bright idea in my head that I needed to get away from home. Graduation from High School had come a few months earlier, and I'd continued to work at a fast food restaurant and attend college. I'd started to work as soon as I could; so, I could help my Mom. She worked hard and supported us four kids. My mother always made sure we had food to eat, lights to turn on and clothes on our back. We, my siblings and I didn't learn about her struggle until, much later.

I didn't make much money where I worked, but I knew it would help her. So, I would take a little, and give her the rest, hoping somehow I could help make her life a little easier. She never talked about the bills, nor did she ever ask for anything from any of us, but I knew she needed help. My parents had divorced when I was younger, and I saw how hard my Mom worked and how tired she was when she came home from working all day.

I, too, had become tired. I felt trapped, working and going to school. I'd seen this story before, and I wanted something different out of life. Truthfully, I was not looking for an adventure; I was looking for a dream, a way to escape. It was courage that rose up in me that challenged me to change and a simple dare that caused me to stop at the Air Force recruiting office and fill out papers to join the military.

8

FREEDOM…?

Stepping into a new-found freedom, I started life on my own. Surrounded by the prayers of my Mother and family, I journeyed to a new city, a new job and a new identity. For a brief moment, I could see a better day emerge. I discovered a new way of living. I breathed in the fresh air of this new city, San Antonio. Lackland Air Force Base! Basic training! I was so scared! Not knowing what to expect, I kept quiet and maintained my composure. I had no ideas, no real thoughts, of what I had gotten myself into.

The Air Force Recruiter probably told me I'd passed the test and the things I needed to do to prepare for basic training. Truthfully, I hadn't listened past the point of "you have passed the test!" Hustle and bustle to prepare for my new future! Clothes to pack, goodbyes to say and my first airplane ride! As the day dawned to leave, I said goodbye to my Mom and family Before the sun had risen, I was picked up by an Air Force recruiter and whisked away to the Military Entrance Personnel Station (MEPS) to take a test and be sworn in. Afterward, we made our way to the Airport, and off to Basic Training!

Once we arrived in Texas, we collected our things and were herded to a bus for a trip to Lackland Air Force base for Basic training. I was scared and excited! It was my turn to get off the bus! I was so excited I didn't see the asphalt rising to greet me! Now that is what I call a welcome! I'd passed out! It was mega hot, humid and my body could not handle the heat. I awoke shortly thereafter with a Drill Instructor yelling in my face!

"Get up you lazy-----! What do you think this is? A resort!" The instructor barked in my ear. "Somebody give her some water!"

This guy was really funny. He needed a stress reliever – I thought to myself as I picked myself up off the asphalt.

Talk about adjusting! I never knew I could move so fast! Here is the funny part, this was kids' play compared to what I'd left back home! I couldn't feel the fear in my heart nor in my soul. I gave him little thought. I was so excited to be starting over!

Okay, I was not that excited about starting over, because I was still woozy from hitting the pavement face first upon arrival! My thoughts were a little muddled. And what made things even worse was, not that I was trying to stick out, I packed too many clothes! The Training Instructor had us open our suitcases on our cots; so, they could check the contents. By the time he got to mine, he was so upset, he was about to explode, because someone packed an alarm clock and a teddy bear! Boy, this is going to be great! I was thinking, these people are hilarious!

After our "meet and greet," all our clothes, suitcase, stuffed animals, and the alarm clock were thrown in a closet along with everybody else's stuff from our flight.

Despite being surrounded by many new faces and new experiences; the dark mass of fear was ever present. I chose to ignore it when it reared its unforgettable presence at any moment's notice. Now on my own, away from family and friends the fear of being alone, not fitting in, or just plain old not being good enough engulfed me. Fear had chosen to return to remind me that I was not alone. Fear was my shadow and once again, my best friend.

Being brave, I tried not to notice that "my friend" was with me. Focusing on exactly what I was told to do, I kept my head above water and out of trouble. Fear was with me on this journey, however he'd successfully hidden away in the corner of my heart, but rearing up at his discretion. He definitely rose up when it was time to go to the chow hall to eat.

We had to walk in front of the Training Instructors' tables. Every day they chose to pick on someone about something. Maybe it
was the way we dressed or how we looked. They even picked on what us about what we were going to eat! Every day I prayed they would not stop me for any reason. Quickly, I would get my food and rush to my

table and sit down. Watching from afar, I saw how embarrassed new recruits were standing before the "elite" Air Force – one explaining why there was cake on his tray while he was overweight. The person was not overweight, but basic training was more about a mind game than anything else. It's amazing I did not get recycled, pushed back a week or two, for laughing at the antics of those in charge.

As a soldier in the Air Force, structure and discipline were strong forces for me. These two things kept me grounded. The first few weeks of basic training were hard, especially when the Training Instructor made me talk to inanimate objects like lockers! If I didn't focus, or if I missed anything, there I was getting yelled at and told to talk to a wall, a locker or a pole –relentlessly reciting whatever ridiculous statement the TI 'politely' told me to say, like "Airman Basic Washington reports as ordered, Sir!" Over and over!

Yelling in my face did shock me back to the present. However, it was hard not to laugh, I managed though. Dogged determination to finish and do whatever it took to get me back on track to finish the course was what I did. Quickly, I learned to focus on what was being taught, stand still in line and eat quickly.

I'd learned early on to be invisible and unseen; this is what I was good at. Since I already believed I was nothing and a nobody, it served me well in this time of my life to be invisible! I was a good soldier! Everything that was asked of me, I did it. I learned what I needed to learn. I jumped when I was told to jump. I did not complain to the TI. I just took whatever was dished out to me.

Life was quite amusing at this juncture. Ladies in my flight were crying, because they had to hold their arms out by their side in a training exercise. I was like, what? You have got to be kidding! I am so glad I did not bust out laughing. I know I would have been recycled, pushed back to day one of basic training!

Having found this new-found freedom, I did some silly things, like standing as a road guard in traffic too long and getting left by my squad, or being disobedient, which caused me to be on lock down in my room for a weekend or two.

After Basic Training and Technical School, I went to my first duty station at Luke Air Force Base in Arizona. I was stationed there for almost five years. While there, I met and married my first husband and had my first child. Unfortunately, we were only married for three years. After our divorce, I was re-stationed in Korea for a year, and then I was sent to an Air Base in Alaska.

Remembering how I got to Alaska, it is safe to say God has a great sense of humor! It began with my best friend, K., telling me she was going to Alaska. At the time, we were living in Arizona. When she told me, she was moving to Alaska, I put in a request to move to the great Northern state. I DID NOT know anything about Alaska. All I knew was that my best friend was going to be there! So, I put in for the overseas assignment, and lo and behold (drum roll please) I got the assignment! My best friend would be in Alaska, and I was going to be in Alaska! This meant I would not be alone. I would know someone!

YES! I was so excited; I couldn't wait to tell her. I stopped by her house on my way home from work and shared the awesome news. Now you would think that my buddy, my ace, would jump for joy! No, that is not what happened! After I shared the assignment selection with her, she was happy for me. But when I excitedly said we will both be in Alaska, the look on her face said something totally different!

"I never told you I was going to Alaska!" She said.

My jaw hit the floor! She kindly, in sincere animation, explained to me that she said she was going to California, not Alaska. Mulling this over in my head, my heart broke. Where in the world was Alaska?! What is Alaska! I am not joking when I say I did not know anything about this state, nor did I have any desire to find out. In that very moment, I knew my life was about to change. Later, I discovered God had a plan, and I was the main character, right smack dab in the middle of a madcap story! This is where the life changing adventure began for me.

Alaska is where I truly met God. It was He who orchestrated this trip to Alaska. In obeying the orders on this new journey, I'd said yes to His plan for my life. Although this leg of the trip was hard on my heart, it caused me to look in the mirror and evaluate who I was, authentically. I had the daunting task of learning to accept myself. For so many years, I had survived by living outside of myself, not acknowledging my own existence. From my own perspective, I had been an outsider and a spectator in my own life. As I said before this type of behavior will catch up with you sooner rather than later.

If anyone knows anything about Alaska, it has very short days in the winter, and this season lasts an average of six months. I survived one day at a time and did not give any real thought to the days ahead.

This place is like none other, unique in its pristine beauty, towering mountains, lush landscapes in the summer and golden leaves cascading from trees in the fall. But that is not what it looked like in the winter when I first arrived at this upper Northern state. It was 1992, and there had been a beautiful snowfall and volcanic eruption that spewed ash across the city of Anchorage, the day before I arrived. Oh, my gosh! It was extremely dirty! And my attitude matched the fallen gray ash that tarnished the white purity of the snow. I was so angry! I could have spit nails! But it was all part of God's plan to change me from the inside out.

From the day I stepped off the plane, I literally hated Alaska! Everything was a complete mess. It was dark and gloomy, and the weather was unforgivingly cold.

Initially, although I was in the military, when I arrived in Alaska, I did not have an official job assignment. I was given menial tasks to complete until a job was located for me. A constant scowl of non-appreciation was the consistent mask on my face. This only made me look worse, and encouraged people not to approach me nor get to know me. I had a nasty attitude to match. I complained and griped and wished I was not located in Snow City Central. However, to no avail, I was not picked up by a heavenly host of angels nor whisked away to a sunny land, far, far away!

Driving at night was a big no, no in my book. I only went out as needed. But sometimes you will do things to find a way out, a way of change without realizing what you are doing. I decided to go to church on a New Year's Eve after trying to party at a local celebratory event to bring in the New Year. To me, this party just fell flat, as I saw the same people I always saw weekend after weekend of partying. These weekend excursions had become a nightmare, and I needed a fresh change.

Feeling exhausted and in need of something new and different, I longed for myself to be changed. I wanted peace within my soul. Blaming others for my poor behavior was completely ludicrous, especially since I was the common denominator.

After being at the New Year's Eve party for an only short while, and twenty-five dollars later, I left. I got into my car and drove around until the idea came to me to go to church. I was dressed in an evening gown with makeup and hair to match. I actually looked like "Princess Barbie." I came to the church on base, and I slipped, unnoticed, into a testimony service at the chapel. I sat in the back hoping that no one would see me.

I'd come searching for something that I couldn't find at the party. I began to listen to the testimonies of the people there. Even though they spoke with joy and great thankfulness, their words could not penetrate the hardness of my heart. Sadness permeated my soul.

I doubted what I was looking for would be found here, but I knew church was where I could find hope. Hope that would calm the raging monster inside of me and bring peace.

It seemed no one said anything or even really took notice of me. Feeling hopeless and without direction, I left the Chapel in tears, and headed home. I slipped out as quietly as I had come in.

Black ice covered the road. I couldn't see it as I drove, but it was there. And so was fear. I'd packed him away, in my heart. He was there waiting for opportunity to get out. He would soon have his chance to make an appearance.

It was a cold, snowy winter night, and I was tense with fear, unable to neither see nor sense what was ahead. The road was dark and slippery. My vision was clouded by tears, and I did not want to spend another minute with this heaviness in my soul, nor did I want to be a part of the party scene. My soul cried for peace as tears of loneliness flowed freely from my burning red eyes.

Suddenly, I jerked back to reality as I hit a patch of ice and the vehicle began to slide out of control! Lost in my thoughts, I had not noticed the black ice on the road! I was in a sideways skid! To the right of my vehicle loomed the tops of trees and a drop off several feet. Terrified, I screamed out to God, as I tried to correct the steering wheel to go in the direction I wanted it to go to no avail. It would not budge!

Suddenly, it seemed as if time slowed down. I clearly saw people, with looks of terror on their faces, drive by in slow motion as I continued to slide towards my death! Before my eyes my very life flashed! Helpless and terrified, there was nothing I could do! Suddenly, my car miraculously came to a stop at the edge of the precipice! Shaking with fear and adrenaline, I put the car in reverse, to clear the edge, set the gear in drive, got back on the road, and drove home very slowly.

Gathering my thoughts, I realized that I was worth saving; I am not alone. Life is bigger than I presumed it to be, and I had to get it together and move forward with a positive outlook on life. I knew I had to change the way I lived, what I did and who I associated with. Raise your hand if it all magically changed overnight? Nope. Not here either.

However, true enough, you will not have to have a death-or-life experience to come to know these things. Take a moment and assess your life. Think about the things you can be grateful for. Write them down and begin to say out loud that you are thankful for these things, one by one. **BE GRATEFUL**…

The next leg of my journey was one of awareness. It was an awareness that was more to life than just me, my problems or situations. The realization that the universe was huge and there was someone watching over me. I was surrounded by a great peace. Still shaken by the life changing almost-drove-off-the-cliff event, the almost-tragic scenario played over and over in my mind. I got home, climbed into bed and cried myself to sleep. The next few days were a complete blur.

Gradually, I got over the shock of "death was upon me syndrome." Saved by an unseen force, something within me awakened. Clawing at the inner core of my being, it had opened my eyes to the possibility of better is possible. Strange enough, I only became angrier at life and myself.

"Why?" You may ask.

There was no answer in my vocabulary or mindset. Mindlessly, I tugged at the visage of hope, grasping the tail end of what possibly could be. Depression now had been added to my repertoire. People annoyed me at every turn, everything seemed dark and dim. So, called "friends" began to call me names behind my back. Nothing felt right. It seemed things were coming full circle again, though I did not care.

Fear's tentacles still clutched my heart – a cold aching heart full of despair. Yet, something within me struggled to live, to breathe. It fought against everything within me to make itself known. Outwardly, I longed for more than what the world could offer. Misery had made its home in my soul, and this void in my heart could not be filled. I'd become miserable, depressed and lonely.

One day, as I was getting ready for work, I suddenly felt overwhelmed by life. I realized it was impossible to fill the empty space within my soul by myself. People and things could not and would not fill the void. These things only offered a temporary solace.

That night, in my deepest slumber, I had a dream. I dreamt a dream so real, I still remember it so very vividly today. Dressed in a white, full-length night gown, I felt I was pulled by my arms and by my feet. At my head appeared three angelic creatures dressed in white. Their faces strained with effort as they pulled my arms with all their might! At my feet, were not so lovely creatures pulling my legs as clouds of darkness encircled them. With yellow and red eyes, they snarled at me, but I sensed they could not harm me. These creatures were covered in darkness, but I could still make out their hideous reptilian-like forms.

"She is mine!" They kept saying, "she is mine!"

I was terrified! I knew, right then and there, I had to make a choice. I cannot say someone tapped me on the shoulder and told me exactly what to do. Nor did God instantly appear and say, "Davina, here are three principles and five points on what you need to do."

No, it did not happen that way. In my gut, my instinct, in this dream, I knew what I had to do. In that moment, I would have to make a decision that would change my life forever. I called a name – a name that heralds the universe, the only name that could save me, "Jesus."

Instantly, the pulling and the tugging ended! I fell to the floor! One second I was on the floor; the next, I was standing in front of a sliding glass door. On the other side was a beautiful light with immense, white clouds and so much peace. I didn't see anyone; I just knew that this is what I wanted and what I needed.

Then I awoke with a start! Something was different. It was not over. I had to make an official acceptance of what I wanted to do. With a loud voice, I cried out to God to help me!

The crossroad was still set before me. I would either go on doing what I'd been doing, or I could choose a different path – a path that would take me to a new life. It would be an adventure that would eventually change the selfish and frightened way I had lived my life.

Having tasted God's sweetness of love and acceptance, my soul craved that feeling again. I'd first tasted the goodness of the Lord in a small church in Arizona. In this place, I experienced the true love and acceptance of a Good Father. Knowing what I wanted could not be found with work, people or things. Crying out with the cry of a soul that was perishing, dry, thirsty, and tainted with shame, my soul longed to be filled with the Presence of God. I screamed and yelled! My heart ached for His presence.

On my way to work in my little red car, little did I know, the God of the Universe, my Abba, had heard my cry, and He would answer my prayer. I would have an experience like never before.

9

WHAT IS FAITH?

HEBREWS 11:1 NKJV – Now, faith is the substance of things hoped for the evidence of things not seen. "Faith is the ability to move forward without seeing the end result – in spite of what is happening or not happening, moving in the unseen realm of belief, knowing that situations will change regardless of what it may look like currently, having a personal vision to ascertain the projected path to be taken, having no fear in delving into the unknown to create a life of abundance."

"Go to church," a small voice said with great authority. So strong, yet so peaceful, I could not resist. There was no strength remaining in me to resist. Suddenly, a picture of a church popped in my head. I knew where to go. I'd been attending Lighthouse Christian Fellowship, a local church off and on. The people were great, and I knew they cared a great deal for me. Fear, on the other hand would not let me connect to my newfound friends. Believing that they did not really care me, kept me away from what could have been mine all along. My church attendance was really poor, and I did not fully believe people so nice could really exist.

"They must have something under their sleeves. They couldn't possibly care for me this much," were my thoughts.

Every time I would see the Pastors wife, Sister Deb, she'd always show me love, kindness and friendship. I'd go to church at her every invitation. I would attend for two to three services, but then I wouldn't be seen again for weeks and months at a time. It was a yo-yo process. But now the yearning to be free had overtaken me. The taste of freedom was right at my fingertips. I knew where to go, and I went that night.

Pastor Ken, gave an altar call, and I quickly went to the altar. Silently, I cried, but I could no longer hold back the torrent of tears that gushed from my eyes nor the sorrow that poured from my heart. As I stood at the altar, nothing mattered. Relationships, the desire to be loved, the cold, the darkness… nothing mattered. Freedom from the darkness and loneliness within was what I wanted. Peace was what I needed. I'd fought against myself, God, and all those who wanted to help for far too long. I'd held on to the weight of fear for far too long in hopes things would somehow get better.

When I chose to commit my life to Jesus, I felt the heaviness of fear, depression, loneliness, masks, and anger literally vanish.

I literally heard the chains I'd carried for years drop from my shoulders. Instantly, I felt extremely light as if a ton of bricks was lifted off them. Every care, fear, rejection, negative thought, or experience left me! I felt light as a feather!

The joy that engulfed me was unbelievable! I knew I would never be the same again! Crying with tears of joy, I wanted to dance, and play and sing like never before. The next day, at work, I told all my friends about Jesus! Young and old alike. Whoever, it didn't matter. Friends dropped me like I had some kind of contagious disease; I was too "out there" for them. But I was free! In order for me to be completely free I had to be delivered from stinking thinking!

In order for me to change the way I thought, I had to change my mindset. My mind had previously been locked in the box of fear. My belief system had to be retrained to believe better is possible.

I have learned fear will keep you in a place of your past – past hurts, past mistakes, past life – if you let it. It will keep you in the arena of doubt, unbelief and not moving forward. Fear's purpose is to keep you "stuck like chuck" for an eternity, if you let it rule your life.

However, faith will propel you into greatness, your purpose and your destiny. It will clarify your identity and lead you on the path you are destined to take. Faith will cause you to believe and do the impossible!

"Greater is He that is in you than he that is in the world," (1 John 4:4).

10

THE POWER OF FAITH

As I began on this new journey of life, God sent an earthly angel to become my best friend and, eventually, my husband – Michael, a kind and gentle man who understood me and loved me in spite of my hang-ups. He carries a great authority and is quite fearless, yet he loves God with all His heart.

Michael proposed to me at the same church where I found my Savior. He proposed in front of the entire church on a New Year's Eve. We were married a short four months later in a beautiful church, surrounded by family and friends. Sometime later, I discovered another wonderful surprise! I was pregnant! I couldn't believe it! I'd been married only a few months, and here I was pregnant! Excitement began to build within me as I thought of the joy of life growing inside me! I was carrying our child! A very special treasure! My husband, Mike, and I had not talked about children right away, but here we were. I never dreamed life could be so good!

I had no symptoms of pregnancy. I just couldn't quite figure out why it was that every time I ate my clothes got really tight. I decided to take a pregnancy test, and it immediately resulted in a positive outcome. Boy was that a shock! Totally unexpected.

As active-duty personnel, I continued to work. I got through the long days of working, thinking of my son, Michael. Every day at noon, I would go downstairs to the basement at work, where the vending machines were, and get a cranberry grape drink. Baby Michael would kick and jump at the pleasure of me drinking the cool refreshing drink. He truly enjoyed this daily routine.

As I grew larger, I began to wear maternity clothing, and people noticed the change. I was so happy. Regular maternity checkups revealed the baby was healthy, with no problems what so ever.

At one of my normal doctor's appointments, I talked to my doctor about not being able to sleep well at night, and he gave me pills to take at bedtime; so, I could rest. I took them upon returning home and fell asleep in an awkward position. Upon awakening, something felt wrong. Little Mikey was not active. He'd stopped moving. It felt as if he were not there.

When my husband came home, I told him how I felt, and he assured me that everything would be okay. We called the doctor and were instructed to come in the next day. Mike and I had been praying, and we'd called the church to pray in agreement with us for our son. Everyone was praying for the best.

We left the next day for the appointment and waited with barely any time to see our doctor. He did an ultrasound and examination and sadly informed us our son had passed.

I couldn't believe it, nor could I accept it. I was a woman of faith, and this just could not be happening.

My mind went back a few months earlier, before I was even married. I was in attendance at our church Saturday morning prayer session, and I'd been praying for quite some time. Suddenly, my prayers changed, and I began to pray and weep as if I was grieving. The cries came from the pit of my soul; I wailed uncontrollably. Eventually, with great exhaustion I literally just laid down on the floor, weeping until I slept.

I understood at that moment in the hospital that I'd previously mourned my son. I'd cried the cry of someone who'd lost a loved one so close to my heart, and I had not even met him yet.

I refused to believe my son was gone. I could not accept it. The next day I was admitted to the hospital to induce labor. My body would not reject my baby; it was as if it clung to the child, not wanting to let go. My stomach had gone slack from the weight of the baby. As the oxytocin, medication to help induce labor, was introduced into my system, my body still refused to react to the drug.

An hour or two passed. The medical staff knew the baby had to be delivered; or it would be detrimental to my health. Hours after increasing the dosage of the medicine, my body reacted, and I delivered our beautiful baby boy. He was six months old, and he was covered in fine hair, with a head full of black curly hair. He was the spitting image of his dad.

The doctor allowed us to say goodbye, before they whisked him away. He was so beautiful and perfectly made. I was in a complete daze. All I could think was he was gone. My baby was gone. My heart felt as if it was wrenched from my body. A sound exited from the very core of my being that could not be fully released into the atmosphere. I groaned instead, as the pool of tears gathered in my lap. I cried, because God had let me down.

Even though, I was still under the influence of painkillers, I reconciled that my son was not coming back. My soul dropped to the floor, and I had no strength to rescue it from the grip of death that had taken my child away. I now wanted it to take me too. Depression landed upon my shoulders, engulfing my mind and my soul. I did not want to live. Nothing mattered. Not before, not after, not ever.

To lose a child, is a type of grief that is unexplainable. It cuts into the deepest, most innermost parts of you. Death leaves darkness inside your heart that can only be removed by the pure love of God, Himself. I'd never known pain like this. It was worse than any disease, physical or mental. This grief that enveloped me and became a part of me; it haunted me day and night. There was no disguise, no mask and no pretending. It was blatantly out in the open announcing to the world that death had come to stay.

Even though death assumed it had won the battle, there remained a tiny flicker of hope. This was all the Creator of the Universe needed to lift me up out of the muck and mire.

A few days later, I was released from the hospital, and my husband and friends of the family helped with arrangements for our son's funeral. I remained completely "out of it." I cannot tell you if I ate, who I talked to, nor what I did. I remember the funeral as kind, and gentle words were spoken over my son. My heart was so broken. I never thought I would overcome this battle.

My son was buried in a small plot of ground in downtown Anchorage, Alaska in a quiet cemetery. This had become my child's home – not the arms of his Mom and Dad, but the cold earth would embrace his tiny frame.

Sometime later, I was at home by myself, angry, sad and depressed. I blamed myself for the death of my son. I cried uncontrollably when I was alone, and I tried to keep it together when my husband was at home. It was equally hard on him. He was so strong and loving toward me.

One day after Mike had gone to work, while on the couch asleep, I awoke to see someone sitting on the floor in front of me with her back facing the couch. She seemed to be watching television. She turned and smiled at me and quietly backed out of the room. She was a beautiful, brown skinned woman with shoulder-length, curly hair. She was gorgeous. As she slipped away, I felt within my soul she had been sent to watch over me, to keep me safe. I did not know her name, nor did she speak. She just left upon my awakening. With her task complete, she smiled and was gone. I never saw her again.

The funny thing is, I recognized her as if I'd seen her before. I cannot tell you if this was a real encounter or a dream, but it was real enough for me. I felt great peace as I wondered what transpired, and I eventually drifted back off into a deep sleep. Later that night, after Mike came home from work. We'd eaten dinner and settled in for the night to sleep, when suddenly I heard:

"I HAVE MADE YOU A JOYFUL MOTHER OF CHILDREN."

The voice was loud and clear, and there was no mistake about the message. I'd been drifting off to sleep, when I heard it, after thinking about losing our child again for the thousandth time.

"Mike, did you say something?" I tapped my sleeping husband on the shoulder.

"No," he answered.

"Are you sure?" I asked.

"I didn't say anything." He drifted back off to sleep.

I knew this was a word from the Lord. This Word spoke into the deepest part of my soul and healed the depression, the hurt, doubt and the fears. The power of the spoken promise soothed the ache in my heart and brought a deep healing within.

I did not immediately have a successful pregnancy after receiving this word. Instead, I had several miscarriages. Each loss was unbearable, but something inside of me could not let go of having a child to hold next to my heart, to love. My husband and I believed the promise in spite of what we saw happen to me. It didn't matter what the doctors said, we had a promise from God and decided to stick to the Word of God like never before.

God carried us through it all. We believed and stood our ground! I dug in by faith that God would not lie to me! Every time people turned around I was pregnant again! I felt the pain and betrayal of those I knew who thought I'd gone nuts!

I kept reading and confessing the Word of God over my life, pregnancy, as well as the child I carried after many months of losing several children through miscarriages. I got a hold of the bible and a book by Jackie Mize titled, "Supernatural Childbirth," that was filled with testimonies and scriptures of faith on having great pregnancies and a drug-free childbirth. Eventually, the book's accompanying cassette tape broke, because I listened to it repeatedly. It's amazing the tape player did not catch on fire; I listened to that tape so much!

Regardless of how my mind, heart and soul felt, joy began to ignite in my spirit. I knew I was destined to be a mother again. I couldn't let that go. However, the enemy of my personal promise did not want the Word of God to come to pass in my life.

"You will never be parents again!" The enemy taunted me relentlessly!

It was a long and arduous journey, yet I knew I would have children. This promise, that I would be a joyful mother of children, would carry me through miscarriage after miscarriage, doctor visits, tests, and physical pain. This powerful promise sustained us, my husband and I, until I gave birth to my daughter, born December 15, 1997 – one year and three months from the time of my son's death in September 1996.

11

MAMA's FAITH - LIVING OUT LOUD!

"Ow! That hurt!" She said it felt as if someone had stabbed her with a sharp knife!

Mom knew something was wrong. She was visiting relatives at our annual family reunion in Florida, and the year was 2011. Mama continued to talk and act as if nothing was wrong. Later that night, she examined herself and found several lumps. She hadn´t noticed they were there before. Once she returned home, she went to the doctor and had a mammogram, biopsies and blood tests. The test results came back as possible stage three or four cancer. Later, the doctor confirmed it was breast cancer at the high stage four. Instinctively, she had already known it, but she did not panic.

Mom took chemotherapy treatments in May, April and the first Friday in June. After the ninth treatment, she was feeling fine, but then she had a bad fall and could not get up on her own.

Scheduled to go to the doctor the following Monday, she couldn't walk; so, my sister Anje, the youngest of four children, with whom our Mom lived, called their neighbor to help get Mama into the truck for the ride to the hospital. Mom was admitted to the hospital and discovered she had neuropathy in her feet.

My Mother, Anne, was also a diabetic and had to be mindful of what she ate. The diabetes had taken a toll on her. She had to have tips of her fingers removed, and her feet were sensitive. The chemo turned her skin very dark, and, of course, fear tried to creep in and tell her that her life was over. Instead of giving in to the fear, she called on Jesus and asked Him to take care of her.

She admitted, she couldn't believe it – the fact that she had cancer. Yet, she knew, as a woman of faith, God would not let her down. The Word of God guided her to only believe, and that's exactly what she did. She totally believed, and had total faith in the power of God.

Enduring, or better yet going through, this tough fight has been rough on my Mom. But, through her, I get to see what real faith looks like. I have seen her ups and downs, doctor appointments, and the pain of all of it. However, I haven't seen every detail of what my Mom has experienced, because I live so far away. My siblings have been there, especially, when she needed them most. I visit when I can to spend time with her.

"I'm fine," she says when I talk to her and ask how she is doing. She absolutely believes in the healing power of God, and she says she does not want to worry me.

My mother has shown me that faith is real, and God is absolute!

Her favorite song is "What God Has for Me Is for Me." Can you imagine the power of God that flows through her? She says if she could give a smile or a kind word, then it's all worth it. My mother's measure of faith is absolutely incredible! Her faith crushes the head of the enemy! Changes others' fear to faith! She absolutely amazes me, by her strength and faith in God.

As I sit and write this small portion of her Faith, I look at her and listen to the strength in her voice. In her voice is the sound of thunder, the sound that could tear the enemy of destruction apart. It is the sound of a Warrior, shouting from the top of the mountain that she will not be defeated. It is also the sound of the still small voice that lives within her, telling her, "We will win together. I will never leave you. I will never forsake you. I AM with you."

It didn't matter when she was once again in the hospital; she knew she would fight again and again with her worship and with God on her side – against the medical reports, what her body was telling her, and what people were thinking and saying. She knew, with everything within her, she would win, because she was ready and willing to represent the Kingdom of God and His Son to the world. Deep within her soul, that she has won this fight of faith.

My Mother is the living epitome of preparing for the Kingdom of God and living a life out loud for Jesus. I am so honored to have such a wonderful person as my Mother. What she has taught me to believe, at all costs, is to let nothing stand in your way. Faith is not based on what we see, hear or feel.

Mama is still with us today. Her cancer is in remission, and the pain is there from diabetes, but she praises through the pain. Even though her journey is not easy, she has already declared the victory. Her reward shall be great. Because of her, my belief in the power of God and His love for us has grown astronomically.

12

WORD OF ENCOURAGEMENT

I encourage you; don't give up. Keep believing, no matter what storms life may bring. The Word says, "Now the just shall live by faith," (Hebrews 10:38). We are not moved by what we see, feel or even what we experience in this long journey of life. We must continue to trust in God by standing on His word through the power of prayer, praise and worship.

The bible says praise stills the hand of the enemy. Here, the word "still" means to desist or to cease. Open your mouth, and let the praise come forth. Release your highest "praise" into the atmosphere, and see the salvation of God.

I choose to praise Him in my dance and shout hallelujah at the top of my lungs to declare the victory is won! I decree and declare my Mother is healthy, healed, whole, and walking in divine health. I decree and declare God's creative power is working on my

Mother's health for a supernatural miracle! She shall live and not die, and she will declare the works of the Lord! For God is her mighty strong tower! He is her deliverer and her strength! It is in Him she lives and moves and has her being!

All of this has happened so souls will be saved, delivered and set free for the advancement of God's plan in this realm. Thank you, Mama, for speaking an "OUT LOUD," message for the Kingdom of the Most High God.

13

THE PROCESS OF DELIVERANCE

My faith walk was not easy. Over 20 years of pain, shame and rejection had to be undone. Deliverance was the only way I could be truly set free. That is how all the chains of my soul had to be removed. The enemy of my soul, my greatest adversary, wanted to destroy my identity, and he nearly succeeded.

Acknowledging I needed help and could not win at life on my own nor on my own terms, and accepting that help, was the greatest step I ever took.

I had been so full of pride. Admitting I did not have it all together was the first step. Walking by faith required I stay in the Presence of the Lord. I had to develop a lifestyle of worship. Surrendering my life to the One True Living God, King Jesus, I gave Him the reigns to do with my life as He pleased.

In other words, I had to change what I'd been doing, and this change in my actions could only happen as I allowed my thoughts to be guided by God's love and not by fear, anger or anxiety.

I was now privy to a beautiful and lasting, relationship with Jesus Christ that I'd never had before. I needed Him more than the air that I breathed.

As I began to see the move of God in my life, I saw Him in the sunrise, the smile of a baby, and He lived in my heart. I knew something was different about me, about life. People looked different; I began to see the goodness in people that I'd never noticed before. It was as if a veil of darkness was removed from my eyes and my heart.

Matthew 5:43-44 (AMP) states, "You have heard that it was said, you shall love your neighbor, (fellow man), and hate your enemy. But I say to you love, (that is, unselfishly seek the best or higher good for) your enemies and pray for those who persecute you. This was the beginning of my deliverance.

I was falling in love with the Lord. I wanted to be where he was, consumed by His presence. In this new adventure, I began recalling instances in my life that brought me to the brink of destruction only to be saved by God's grace – people who'd hurt me in the past and things I'd done to hurt others. As these things were systematically brought to my remembrance, I had to forgive them, but I also had to forgive myself.

The realization of what I'd done and who I'd become brought me to my knees. I was taken aback by the vileness of my ways. The stench that protruded from my soul must have been foul to the nostrils of my Savior; however, He still accepted me into His arms. He embraced me with a purity of love I'd never known:

a strong and loving embrace that any little girl wants from her Daddy. With that embrace, my heart melted, and I could feel the love of my heavenly Father pour into me.

It was an uneven exchange, my filth for His best, Himself. You must understand; this is all I had to give. Turning over what darkened my soul was all I had to give. I literally saw the pain upon the heart of my Father caused by the years He'd waited for me to open my heart to Him. My heart dropped to the floor, and I cried as I released the weight of what I had carried for so long. In that moment, I decided I wanted to be free, and I accepted the pure and holy love of the Father in exchange for the evil that had lurked in my heart.

The process of deliverance was not an easy one. There were things I had to let go, that I'd clung to and accepted as a part of my identity, such as pride, selfishness, hate, fear, and unforgiveness. However, when you look in the mirror and the Lord shows you a better you, those things of the past do not matter. You become a new creation in the Lord!

Initially, I prayed to be more like Jesus. At church, I began to establish a relationship with people who genuinely cared about my wellbeing. Studying the bible also changed the way I thought about life. Instead of seeing things based on what I could get out of them, I began to desire to know how I could help others. As my prayer life grew, I began to pray for those who'd hurt me in the past.

Forgiving myself was one of the hardest things to do. I'd never heard of forgiving yourself for anything. I understood the reason why I could do this was because I'd acknowledged I was not perfect and I'd made mistakes.

As I thought about my past, pictures of people who'd abused me, beaten me, betrayed me, or even used me flashed across my mind. I forgave them. I decided to no longer give them power they never deserved. They could not have authority over my life any longer.

I admit; at first, it felt like I was saying it was my fault that they hurt me. Yet, it was not my fault. I realized I had been "easy pickings" for some and for others a way to let off a lot of steam. I had been the victim, but I had chosen not to remain that way. I chose to change – to not only help myself, but to help others as well.

My heart was changing. I knew it when I looked at people who I disliked, and seeing them did not bother me. The Lord allowed me to see people through His eyes. For instance, there was a lady I used to work with who had it in for every woman at the workplace. I saw her and the hurt that was in her eyes, and I began to pray for her. I prayed that God would heal her heart and help her not be lonely. She eventually moved on, and I'd thought I'd never see her again.

Sometime later, I saw her, and she gave me a hug. I was truly shocked! She seemed genuinely happy to see me! We chatted for a little while and parted ways. The change in her was very visible. I'm sure there were others who also prayed for her, and that helped to heal her heart. The hurt that was so evident in people lay heavy on my heart. I prayed for them, and I believed God for their "Deliverance", as I continued to fellowship with the Lord in prayer.

He began to show me things about myself that needed to be changed. In my heart, there was the pain of abuse, rejection and fear. I'd decided to stay at the church where I'd given God my life. Here I found the love, hope and courage I was looking for. I'd found people who accepted me as I was, scars and all. There was real love here. I didn't have to look any further, I'd found my home.

My Pastor taught the Word of God in power! His messages of faith encouraged my spirit and my soul. I was so hungry for the Word of God; I fiercely consumed the words he spoke.

"Faith is the substance of things hoped for the evidence of things not seen," (Hebrews 11:1).

Learning about faith caused me to think differently. I believed for the impossible! Serving on several ministries in the church brought me closer to Jesus. In my new church home, I was introduced to the ministry of Dance.

When I was out in the world, all I wanted to do was dance. I even ended up on a Dance Television show in Arizona! It was so much fun! Dancing the night away brought me freedom. I could out dance anyone! Many of my dance partners would walk away sweaty and tired, leaving me on the dance floor wondering what was wrong with them. Often, I would stay until the lights came on and had to be ushered out. Lo and behold, I was out again the next weekend dancing the night away.

However, as a newly saved person, I really didn't think about dancing; my heart was satiated with the presence of the Lord. I'd grown tired of seeing the same people night after night. Going out to clubs grew stale and old. This new life didn't call for anything old and dry, and the truth is, dancing never crossed my mind. That is until someone asked me what I liked to do.

The scene goes like this: the praise and worship team was having a meeting. I was a newbie to the team; so, I didn't feel I had anything to contribute. All this "Christian" stuff was new to me. When the question was asked, "who used to go out and dance all night?" Of course, I raised my hand with great enthusiasm. I'm not sure why the question was asked, but I answered a resounding, "I DID!"

I'd given up my old life; so, I could start fresh and new. As a young child in church, my Mother was an "every Sunday attendee" and would help put together the church programs for Easter, Christmas and Mother's Day. She also assisted with the kid's choir, cooked in the kitchen and did many other things in the church. She made sure her kids participated in the ministries at church. This built a rich heritage for me, as the church was the backbone of our family growing up.

I sang in the choir, worked on the children's usher board, and participated in the Easter and Christmas programs. I remember one Christmas we kids danced to "O Holy Night." We worked hard to learn the dance steps! After much practice, the day of the event came. It went off without a hitch! It was a very beautiful dance. I can still remember parts of the dance to this day. Answering that one dance question with a resounding "Yes" set me on a journey to total freedom.

14

DANCING INTO FREEDOM

The year was 2001, and I'd seen my first liturgical dancer who danced under the power of the Holy Spirit. I was completely mesmerized. She danced with beauty and grace. I'd never seen anything so magnificent in my entire life. Sure, I'd seen the Alvin Ailey Dance Company and dreamed of being a part of this prestigious dance troupe. However, this dancing was different.

I saw the beauty of God shine down upon the young lady as she danced! I could hardly stay in my seat! I saw something that caused my heart to leap in my chest! It was as if time stopped, and she and I were the only two people in the room. Her praise dance was amazing!

After the program was over, I rushed backstage and burst into her dressing room. She looked at me with great surprise, as I blurted out I wanted to do what she just did. I think she thought I was totally crazy.

Looking back on that moment, I'm sure I looked a little kooky around the edges!

She shared with me her name, Renee Gray, and gave me her phone number. We promised to stay in touch, and we did. We got to know each other, and she eventually became my friend, mentor and dance coach.

When Renee opened a Praise Dance School in Alaska, I was excited to attend. She taught praise dancing according to the Word of God, ballet 101, choreography and so much more. However, there are some things that cannot be taught but only caught. With Lady Renee, and the dances she taught me, a whole new world opened to me.

In addition to my church teaching me about faith, prayer, praise, and forgiveness, Lady Renee also taught me about worship in the dance. Worship was the key element to my deliverance and healing. It drew me into the arms of my Father and kept me there. When things became overwhelming, I knew I could depend on the Lord to draw me out of my funk.

Eventually, I joined an intensive, one-year dance program titled: The Eagles International Training Institute Dance Year One, spearheaded by Dr. Pamela Hardy. This program was life-changing. I look back on that time and know that if I had not had this course, I'm sure I would not be where I am today.

When I became the Dance Team leader at my church and needed guidance on the ministry of dance, I sought the Holy Spirit and asked Him, "How do you dance in church?"

I knew nothing about dance in the church. The Holy Spirit specifically told me that we would start with

"Sign Dance." I was like, "what?"

He told me where to go to buy the book for sign language and begin there. I asked people at church if they would be a part of the team; they agreed, and so the dance of life began. Dancing became my personal language to God. Morning, noon and night His love and grace poured through me. It was so very exciting to be a part of something so alive and vibrant!

Dancing became my prayer to the Father as I lavished him with my love. Kneeling, spinning, and jumping, I danced until I could dance no more. Pouring out my soul to him is what I lived for.

"Faith, the epicenter of your dreams and visions, will cause you to walk a million miles, just so you can reach your Destiny..."

Davina Stallworth

15

INTO THE NEXT DIMENSION – LOVE CONQUERS ALL...

"Shift into the next dimension of freedom and out of the futility of fear. Shift into faith, into the atmosphere of My greatness that I have already planned for you. I have set you here in this realm to be a light in a dark and dying world. I have set you here to gather My sheep. I have not given you a spirit of fear, but a (spirit of) power, love and a sound mind.

"I have raised you from amongst them. I have trained you for war. I have trained you for battle. Do not be easily beset by sin. You are the generation I have called out to take over and conquer the kingdom of darkness. Do you not know I am here to keep you, guide you and protect you? My love will surround. My love will protect you. I will never leave you nor forsake you.

"I knew you before you were formed in your Mother's womb. You are destined for greatness. Now, pick up your plow and move forward. Do not look back, but look forward to the future I have put in you. Open your eye gates and see what I have planned

before you. I AM the God of the impossible. Is there anything too hard for me? Prepare to be shifted and aligned with my plan, sayeth the Lord of Host!

"I will bless those who bless you and curse those who curse you. I have called you to be a vessel of my pure and holy love. I have called you to be a vessel of my joy and laughter. Joy because you bring great joy to My heart, and laughter because you will see and laugh at the plans of the enemy.

"Adapt and align to My way of doing things. Be no longer hindered by fear! I release you and cause you to step boldly into the calling upon your life. I will always love you. I will never leave you. Hold onto these words for they are health and life to your flesh."

Shifting required I be released from the futility of fear. I could not serve the master of fear and walk in faith at the same time. Having two masters would not be permitted in this walk. Now, I'd stepped out in faith, knowing I needed change.

Change came in the form of spending time in communing with the Father through prayer. Change came in the form of praise and worship dance. Change came in the form of being a wife and mother. Wanting change became the faith walk of a lifetime. That is, surrendering to His ways and not my own.

God said in His Word that He is love, and He also said, "Perfect love cast out fear." So, how can these two dwell together unless they agree? Fear cannot agree with love, because fear requires faith in the opposite or absence of what it sees. Fear lives by what it sees in its' mind; it has no hope – only visions of the most terrifying scenarios imaginable.

Meanwhile, love is all consuming. There is no darkness, no hate, no unforgiveness, and no fear in the power of love.

Love consumed and took over my heart and replaced it with a new one, from stone to flesh, so that I could truly live and love again.

Are you shifting into love? It is a choice. It is a matter of changing the mind to believe what is written in the living Word. You must ask yourself, "Do I want to love myself and others? Am I willing to die to self; so that others can receive what rightfully belongs to them?"

I knew I had to answer these questions. It was His blood that dripped from the cross, onto the ground. Blood ran down His face and cascaded beneath His feet. His flesh was marred, bruised, ripped open, and torn to shreds. Jesus was beaten and mocked. His beard was ripped from His face and chin, as the town leaders cried out against Him. A crown of thorns was placed upon His head, to represent our deliverance from any mental anguish. He bore our sickness and disease (see Isaiah 53).

Scourged by the hands of Roman soldiers, Jesus was forced to carry His own cross. At Golgotha, He was nailed to the cross, yet He still clung to the power of Love – a love greater than our own, greater than the whole universe, more powerful than the cruelest heart, but gentler than the sweetest dove. His is a love so pure, it can crumble the highest mountain with a simple word. "For God so loved the world that He gave His only begotten son, that whosoever believes in Him shall not perish but have everlasting life," (John 3:16).

STOP! Take a moment, and allow the love of the Lord to wash over you, change you, and cleanse you.

Close your eyes, and take a deep breath. Focus on Jesus. Focus on what He has done for you...

16

IDENTITY – WHO ARE YOU?

Who am I?

Fear had been my identity. It had become my name, and I had claimed fear as my own. Looking through the eyes of fear caused me to see my identity through tainted, rose colored glasses of shame and rejection.

I had no idea who I was, and I wasn't even looking for her. Surviving was my only goal. I could find her later. It would take years of searching, trial and error to locate the woman I am today. But I am here to tell you, you do not have to go through what I went through. "Six easy steps" is not in my vocabulary; however, I do have a few suggestions to help you discover who you really are.

TAKE A DEEP BREATH...

Do you know who you are? Have you sat down and

asked yourself this question? You are more than the sum total of your past experiences. Who you really are deep down on the inside is waiting to get out. There is greatness in you that is ready to change the world! Take a deep breath and think about what you like to do best.

Christ asked the question, "who do you say I am?" The Apostles responded with their appropriate answers, but there was only one who declared that Jesus is the Son of God. The Holy Spirit revealed this to the disciple.

Who do you say you are? Before you can answer who, you are, you must know that you are here for a reason. Knowing the reason means knowing the what.

God says, "He knows the plan He has for you, plans to prosper you and not to harm you to bring you to an expected end." (Jeremiah 29:11.)

"What am I purposed for?" You will ask yourself this question time and time again. I asked myself this question so many times; my middle name was changed to "who am I?" Ok, just kidding, but nothing came clear until I began to do. Doing things that I'm good at produced the desire to know who I really was and discover my purpose and destiny.

At an early age, my Mom taught me to cook. She would call me into the kitchen to help with Sunday dinner. Hating this chore is not even the correct way to describe this "Mama Time" inflicted trauma. But I learned. I learned to appreciate the dicing of onions and celery to make the dressings for Sunday dinner. I enjoyed making buttermilk cornbread and sweet iced tea.

Watching Mama prepare meals was a real treat, especially when she made her famous sour cream pound cake! We children got to lick the bowl afterwards. There is nothing like my mom's fried chicken. She would season the chicken with salt and pepper, flour on both sides and fry it. Mom's Sunday dinner was the highlight of the week! Macaroni and cheese, collard greens, cornbread, candied yams, a hen, and dressing for dinner. My Mother had a grand appreciation for food and knew how to make every meal special. Even in the special lessons of learning how to cook, it prepared me to know who I am today. I learned to appreciate turning something simple into something deliciously grand.

Knowing the "who" may seem very general. Questions such as: What is your name? What do you like to do? What is your favorite this or that? These may seem very basic.

Let's say, for the sake of an experiment, you are an actor. You've recited a monologue on numerous occasions, and you are moderately good at what you do. So, let's add the "why do you act?" to the equation. What is your reason for acting? Because you love it, and your dying mother asked you to become an actor. Now your monologue takes on a life of its own. Once you discover the "why," your life will never be the same.

In another example, you have been dancing in your church for several years, because you were forced to do so. But as time passes on you discover an intimate relationship with the Lord, Jesus. As you dance, you discover dancing takes on a whole new meaning. The dormancy that had been in you for so long dissipates as you dance before the King of Kings.

In my personal journey of discovering who I really was, I searched among men, seeking approval. I wanted someone else to tell me who I was, despite the Holy Spirit telling me for years who I was. The key ingredient to keeping in what the Lord says you are is to believe.

It doesn't matter what anyone says about you. It doesn't matter whether they believe you or not. The enemy's plan is to kill, steal and destroy, (John 10:10). The enemy's job is to take away your identity by keeping you in fear. Fear will hold you longer than you desire and create an entirely new destiny, a life based on fear, rejection and intimidation.

If you do not jump out of the comfort zone, if you continue to hide your God-given talents and abilities, you will become stagnant.

I remember being terrified of confronting people. I would accept the hairstyle from the hairdresser, though it was not what I wanted. I would accept an order of food, even if it was nasty. Causing waves or confronting situations was not my cup of tea.

One day, at church, my Pastor spoke about confrontation and how to overcome it. Basically, he said you have to confront that which brings you fear. That's what I began to do!

For me, it was not easy. Fear would rise up and literally paralyze me. Enduring the shame of people degrading me was very hard. But as the preacher continued to speak, and I continued studying and reading the Word, I realized something – the fear of people was leaving me. **"Operating in Fear is never the answer to Wisdom." – Davina Stallworth**

17

YOU ARE CREATED FOR GREATNESS

You are Created for Greatness,
No matter what others say!
You are Created for Greatness.
Let nothing stand in your way!
Bow your knee to nothing but God alone.
You see;
You must Seek His Face so early.
For He has come to make you free.
Time to stop doubting;
Accept the faith inside.
The enemy has been telling you
way too many lies!
Your assignment the Lord has given
So that those who are in darkness
Will now begin to see
The hope that is set before them.
Now they can truly be Free.

You are Created for Greatness!
Fear no longer rules your heart.
Time for you to take a stand.
Time to do your part.
You are Created for Greatness.
Let this ring so very true.
Love will conquer all
 And abundant life He has given to you.
Abundant life to the fullest
He has come to give.
Take this message to the world
So that others now may live!

Repeat this message daily –
See it before you Be it!

I AM CREATED FOR GREATNESS

Write down positive thoughts of who you believe you are and the reasons why...

_____

_____

_____

_____

_____

_____

_____

_____

_____

_____

_____

_____

_____

_____

_____

_____

_____

_____

_____

_____

_____

_____

_____

_____

_____

_____

18

SHIFT! FROM FEAR TO FAITH – SPEAK IT OUT!

The Power to Change Your Situation

"Shun profane and idle babblings, for they will increase to more ungodliness," (2 Timothy 2:16, KJV).

"You is smart. You is kind. You is important." These famous words were spoken to the little girl at the end of the movie "The Help," by her caregiver who had just been let go. She'd cared for and protected the little girl. The child had been carelessly talked to as if she was nothing and even ignored as if she did not exist, when in reality the whole world was at her feet. Those few, empowering words spoken by her caregiver had the power to change her life, to set her on a path of possible forgiveness and greatness.

In your mouth, you have the ability to tear down or

build up a person. With spoken words, atmospheres change, hearts are broken, and forgiveness is issued. What words are you holding in your mouth to speak into the person sitting right next to you? You are what you speak, because these words have found a place in your heart. Your heart will carry what your voice speaks.

Have you ever said something about someone, and it came to pass, good or bad? You can choose to speak into the atmosphere what you want to have.

There is an old saying, "sticks and stones may break my bones, but words will never hurt me," that is a complete farce. Earlier in this book, I mentioned some of the hurtful things that were said or done to me when I was a child. There is the power of life and death in the tongue, and we will eat the fruit of what we speak.

The bible says it better this way, "death and life are in the power of the tongue, and those who love it will eat its fruit," (Proverbs 18:21, KJV). Negative speaking brings forth negative things. Positive thinking brings forth positive changes. In order to speak what is good, analyze what you are focusing on.

I am not perfect; therefore, I must watch what I speak. Catching my thoughts and thinking the good things, then speaking the great things, can bring forth the best in me. Practicing positivity and speaking good things have been an adventurous journey for me. Fighting the good fight to maintain my best mindset and succeed in life is what I set my mind and heart to do.

There had been a bad spell in my life when there seemed to be nothing good. The bad decisions and consequences of those choices hounded me day and night. Even when I did not do anything to receive it, the bad spell still knocked on my door, and I gladly opened the door and welcomed it in my life! The door to negative words spoken such as "you are dumb, stupid and ugly;" so that is what I became. Not knowing any better, I acted out those characteristics and behaviors. The truth was I was an extremely intelligent, clever and pretty little girl. However, I was told the opposite day in and day out, and those negative words had seeped into my existence and poured into my everyday life. Those words had cut to the core of my soul, and I believed the lie I was told as a child.

In my mind, I could not see the beauty of God's creation or creativity in me. Seeing the "ugly" was the only thing I knew how to do. The ugly words that were spoken to me became my vision and my truth.

I'm grateful my Mother was a praying Mom. I'm sure that because of her prayers, and those of others like her, my heart changed to become the person I am today. My Mother would say, "If you can't say anything nice, don't say nothing at all."

The Word of God directs us to think on good things. Things that are noble, true, just, pure, and lovely (see Philippians 4:8). The negative words spoken to you are a lie until YOU accept them as truth.

I went through such a hard time; I would not dare believe in me or what I could become. Beyond survival, there was nothing except an everyday existence – not to eat nor sleep – just to survive, to live.

When I was a little girl, I accepted these words in my heart as real, because they were said to me constantly, and therefore, I believed them. My heart carried the lie, and I began to conform to the words spoken over me.

Someone asked me why I did the things that I did.

"Because I'm stupid and dumb," I replied. I became what I believed.

I'm sure there was someone who was speaking words of love and positive affirmation into my life, but it could not override the constant replay of other negative words in my head. The negative replay was more constant than what the "good" words were in my life.

How did I change? Well, I had to change what was put into my head and my heart on a constant basis. I had to change what my eyes were seeing and what my ears were listening to, because these things were ingrained in my life. I had to change what I spoke about myself and look again at who I really was.

Even though I did not have a better vision for myself, I decided to listen and feed on the word of God and apply what I learned. Reading the bible, the word of life and power, gave me insight into who I really was and what I was to become. The Word of God said to me, "Greater is He that is in you than he that is in the world (1 John 4:4).

God has given me the power to overcome any obstacles, because He Himself is in me. I did not have to tolerate the lies that were fed to me, such as "I was nothing and a nobody" or that I would "never amount to anything." I did not have to be afraid.

I CHOSE NOT TO BELIEVE the dark words. I could be strong and courageous in Christ Jesus. I can, and am, more than a conqueror. I choose to believe this about myself despite what the world says about me or even what I look like in the mirror.

Change was coming, and the power of the spoken Word was creating in me a new desire to become someone better. One day at a time, I spoke into existence who I wanted to be, who I was to become. I had to believe with my heart and speak it with my mouth, to change the circumstances that surrounded me. As I started to speak positive words over my life, I did begin to change. The funny thing was, in order for me to change, I had to learn how to see the world differently.

My natural eyes, through which I'd seen myself all my life, had to become something better. I had to have a vision that spoke of God's love and not my own.

"The just shall live by faith, and not by sight," (Romans 1:17).

I had to speak to the storms that surrounded me and tell them to go! As directed by the Word of God, I began to speak to the mountains of fear, doubt and rejection! I did not want these things to be a part of my life any longer. I made up my mind, and therefore I spoke good things. Not fully believing nor comprehending these new, good truths, I spoke anyway.

I did not allow my feelings and emotions to stand in the way of my solid determination to win, and that is when the huge storm of fear began to dissipate. My desire to be better and accept what rightfully belonged to me caused the reality of what I had lived and accepted to be drastically shaken! I had to live, and I had to believe better was possible!

The shining of the glorious sun, that rose every day and provided the light into a magnificent existence, was not just for certain people; it was for me too. I just had to grab hold of the beautiful possibilities before me. Like a carrot placed in front of a race horse, I accepted the challenge and began to run the predestined race set before me!

I had to hang on and run as if my life depended on it! By faith, hope, mercy, and grace I ran for my life by speaking good things! On the next page, you will find words of affirmation to encourage you to step out of the everyday, mundane life into the powerful, abundant life that is rightfully yours. You have the power to speak — use what has already been given to you.

19

CONFESSIONS OF AFFIRMATION:

I AM FEARFULLY AND
WONDERFULLY MADE
I AM BEAUTIFUL
I AM POWERFUL
I AM ANOINTED
I AM GRACEFUL
I AM SMART
I AM INTELLIGENT
I AM LOVE MYSELF
I AM WISE
I AM KNOWLEDGEBLE
I AM PATIENT
I AM A LOVER OF THE CREATOR
I AM INFLUENTIAL
I AM A GO GETTER
I AM A PERSON OF GREAT AUTHORITY

20

SHIFT! FROM FEAR TO FAITH – TRUST

Trust...
"Trust in the Lord with all thine heart, lean not unto thine own understanding, acknowledge Him in all your ways and He shall direct your path..." (Proverbs 3:5-6).

Trust is a very fickle thing. I learned soon enough; I had not completely trusted God. He was supposed to be my everything. Even though I did not fully understand why, I knew this.

The price of trusting is vulnerability, to let yourself be seen for who you really are. Let others see your faults and shortcomings. That is how to know the real you.

Who would want all their dirty laundry aired out in the open? I did not, because boy did I have a lot of laundry piled up! I had to let go of who I thought I was; so, I could be healed and made whole.

Knowing that you need others to help you make it in life and allowing people to help you make it in life are two different things. Letting go and sacrificing your way of doing things takes a lot of courage. Trusting also means you must be aware that you cannot do life on your own. My first step was to acknowledge the needs of others, and my next step was to allow others to be a part of my life.

The bible defines trust as being confident, being sure, and being bold with belief. Trust was not an easy accomplishment for me. It required that the barriers I'd put up be broken down. These barriers were built with blood, sweat and buckets of tears.

How would I begin to trust? After all, I'd had my share of betrayal, deception and lies. Living a life of lies was not as easy as it seemed.

Lies build up and you forget the first one you told to cover up the story you told to make you look like something you are not. After a while, you do not remember what you were trying to do. Lies continue like an endless roller coaster – up, down and even sideways – that is until the roller coaster comes to an abrupt halt! That's when everything tumbles down around you. It never pays to lie.

There were times when things would come out of my mouth that I knew were a lie. The person I was talking to knew it was a lie. Even the people not in the conversation knew I was telling lies. The only thing that stopped me, eventually, was a sermon I'd heard one Sunday morning. By this time, I'd been in the church for a few months, and was hungry for the word of God as well for a difference in my life. My heart was being remolded day by day, to reflect the one who saved my life from destruction.

"Your flesh cares nothing about nothing. It only cares about 'self.' Pleasure and comfort is what the flesh seeks," my Pastor at the time said something to this effect. "It doesn't care; it's going back to dust any way."

Therefore, knowing the carnality of the heart, I had to make a quick-change decision to reset my brain and heart against the way things were going.

Again, to stop doing something that had been ingrained in my psyche as a child, I had to break habits had hindered me from moving forward into making healthy decisions.

21

THE JOURNEY OF FAITH...

The road of faith is not an easy journey. This is not the yellow brick road! The path is filled with twists and turns, lumps and bumps, potholes and stumps. Distractions here and time stealers there! Lord knows you will have your insurmountable share! Roadblocks, popups, pitfalls, and the like! There is no way you can walk this walk with the fallacy of "luck."

Do you know how big a mustard seed is? It is one of the smallest seeds; however, it produces a great big tree! God has said He has given you a measure of faith (see Romans 12:3).

Acts 17:28 states "It is in Him we live and move and have our being." The faith we have been given is not for us, it is for those who need to be healed, who need hope and deliverance (see 1 John 4:17, 3:5).

Even though you are doing what God has called you to do with tears, fear and trembling, persevere, do not quit. Even when it appears nothing is happening, continue to walk in faith. Do not focus on what is before you. Take your eyes off what is wrong, and look at what is right. Focus on the good things about yourself, and watch how your view of life will change and cause good things to be attracted to you.

Let's say your focus is on being beautiful. So, you say: "I am beautiful. I am fearful and wonderfully made." What you focus on is what you eventually become. Eventually, your thoughts and your positive words of confession will drop from your head to your heart, and you will be transformed. The Word of the Lord says, "Be transformed by the renewing of your mind" (Romans 12:2).

If you choose to think about good things, (see Philippians 4:8), this is what you will have, but if you think only about your past, you will stay there and become locked in your past.

Stuck in 1979, wearing bell bottoms and listening to disco music? Does that sound promising? I was scared in this new walk. I was afraid, because I didn't know the will of God. I didn't know what He wanted to have transpire in my life. Yet, I knew I believed in Him and that He His Word spoke the truth and what He says will come to pass.

Be secure in who you are in God. Know your identity. Know God. You must know for yourself the Word of God will not fail. Do not base your faith on what you feel or what you see. Base your faith on your knowledge of God. If you do not know this faith, spend time in His Presence.

Start with thanking Him for what you do have. Thank Him for delivering you out of the hand of the enemy. Thank Him for being alive.

Now is the opportunity to change. It is hard to stand and say, okay Lord, I know You will do it – even though you see nothing to support your belief. It will help you to meditate on the Word, to pray and worship before the King.

When the Lord told Abraham, he would be the Father of many nations (see Genesis 17:4), to look at the stars, that His children would be as bountiful as the stars… Abraham was an old man. Sara, his wife, was past the time of child-bearing. The book of Genesis even talks about how Sara laughed!

Laughter is not what I want to do when I am going through something! I want to cry and just be mad! However, I always come back to Him. I recognize that God is a whole lot bigger than me, and I cannot and will not box with Him.

Isn't it funny how we humans get mad and put up our fist at God, get an attitude and literally throw tantrums when things go awry? We must understand that God already knows what we will go through, and He has a plan. Our job is to seek His face and believe God for an answer or strategy to get through.

I've heard people say God will not "drop it" – your answers or needs – out of the sky. I say, if God wants to drop whatever I am asking Him for out of the sky, I am not going to stop Him! Refusing to put Him in a box is the best way to go! You see; God is faithful to watch over His Word to perform it. (See Jeremiah 1:12)

Where it is impossible with man, it is possible with

God. Examine the story of Mary, the Mother of Jesus, who when she was beyond hope became impregnated with the Messiah, the Son of God.

Jesus, gave His life for us while we were yet in sin – over 2,000 years ago, before you and I were ever thought about – He made a plan for us to gain true freedom, (see John 3:16).

This walk will not be easy, but it will be the best journey you will ever take. Because at the end of the road is a life that is improved by His love. A new life that is now dedicated to living a life of purpose and destiny for the betterment of mankind. As you journey along this path, know that He will never leave you nor forsake you. He may very well carry you on occasion.

Know this: He is the ultimate Father. He knows what is best for you. He is a kind and loving Father who created you from the best there is and ever will be, Himself.

Communication is the key to this journey. Talk to Him; tell God how you feel, what you are going through. Yes, He knows, but it is important to cultivate an active relationship with Him. This relationship is not one-sided. Give Him the time to speak and to share with you not only the plans for your life, but others' lives as well.

I remember, one day I was driving home, and I was having this conversation, not really talking but just thinking, about strawberry shakes.

I said, "I really like strawberry shakes."

Suddenly, I heard this voice say, "I know. I made you that way."

The voice was so audible and clear; it startled me.

I'm surprised I didn't run off the road!

Open your heart to receive His words, believe His heart will connect to yours. Accepting His love is a key component to hearing His voice. God is not going to beat you over the head with a stick if you do something wrong. He expects you to recognize what you've done wrong, repent of your action – that is, to turn away from it – ask Him for forgiveness, and forgive yourself. Perfection is not who we are. We are still children, no matter how old we may be.

"Now Faith is the substance of things hoped for the evidence of things not seen," (Hebrews 11:1).

This road of faith is not for the faint nor the weak minded; you must be aware and strong of heart! A sword and shield you must carry with determination to win and persevere.

The full armor of God you are wearing, and you must move on without a care. The enemy will come to attack you; that will be His stint! Your heart and mind must be on Jesus, and your eyes set like flint. Big steps, small steps; it doesn't matter which. Just keep on moving, just don't lay down nor sit. Know that the plans of God are not for evil but only good. Remember to keep moving forward as a good determined soldier would.

God has promised he'll be with you, day and night, night and day. Keep looking toward the hills, and He will continually guide your way. The journey of Faith is not easy, but there is much wisdom to be gained. Just remember the One who died for you, who hung on a cross and was slain. Keep your eyes on the straight and narrow path; do not look to the right or left.

Treat others with kindness, the strong and the weak. The Lord is always with you; therefore, Him shall you seek. Know that Your past is behind you, and your future is before you. Your journey of faith will take you to the door of opportunities. Listen to wisdom, and faith you must keep. The journey does not last forever, be patient and have peace.

22

SHIFT INTO FORGIVENESS…

Is it simple enough to have faith? To believe in the unseen? Do you believe you have an imagination? Use your God given imagination to change your future to change your life. We are overcomers it is our faith that overcomes the world. The just shall live by faith (see Revelations 12; Romans 1:17).

We cannot be moved by what we see or feel. Here is an example: someone has done something to you or against you, but you choose not to forgive them. Who are you hurting? That person or yourself? Unforgiving is no way to be. It does nothing good for you. The person who hurt you goes on living, and perhaps not even aware of the damage he or she has caused you. Yet, when you choose to hold on to the hurt, anger or hate, these feelings will continue to cause you pain until you release them through forgiveness.

They hurt me. They offended me. They talked about

me. They. Them. Everybody. The hurt is real, and it can last a long time, if you allow it. Can you imagine if you did not forgive people, and they could feel the power of the hurt they caused you? Or they could feel your pain in your heart or your body? Wouldn't that be something? Well, I am here to tell you that they can't.

Most likely, they are not thinking of you. Forgiveness is not meant to make them feel better, though on some occasions it may help those who are actively seeking forgiveness. It is not based on what you feel or don't feel.

Forgiveness is meant to heal your heart.

Your heart may be torn in two, but that does not change the truth that you must be quick to forgive.

"But if you do not forgive, neither will your Father in heaven forgive your trespasses" (Mark 11:26).

Yes, it was horrible what was done to you. True enough, it was wrong, but it is past time to move on from this point in your life. It may not feel like anything new is happening, but this weight will lift from your heart, and the healing process will begin.

If you do not forgive quickly, you will become spiritually stagnant. I don't care how many scriptures you memorize. Even if you are there before the doors of the church are open, and you're on your knees praying on the doorstep. Unforgiveness will kill the body.

When you see people with a frown on their face, who look like they have everything going for them, but they are upset, griping and complaining, it's because they have not let go of a hurt. Unforgiveness does the body no good. The bible tells us to be quick to forgive.

The plan of attack is this: make up your mind that you are valuable and worth more than money can buy. Pray for those who spitefully use you; know that you are not destined to stay in any circumstance unless you decide to stay in it. Praise the Lord as you go through. Yes, it may be hard, but I did it, and so can you.

Stay in the Word; read the Word; memorize the Word; and imagine the Word. See the Word come to life in your situation. Be quick to forgive. Don't allow the enemy to steal your joy, just because you may be in a storm.

Forgiveness is not based on your feelings. You forgive, because you are commanded to "be quick to forgive." The scriptures do not say, you have to have a warm and fuzzy feeling nor that you will receive a grand revelation when you forgive. No, I have had to forgive people, when I did not want to forgive them. They'd hurt me by calling me names or betraying me! They'd hurt my feelings and my pride! How dare God ask me to forgive them! But I understood that Jesus was hurt a whole lot worse than I ever was or ever could be. Jesus endured so much pain, just so I could have an abundant life (see John 10:10).

In my personal walk through this journey, I could not stay in the place of noncompliance. I had to believe what was said in the scriptures was true. Courage, it took courage to live by faith.

I chose to forgive, even though I couldn't see, feel nor hear the change in someone's heart. If I had not forgiven those who had hurt me, I would not have been able to receive the things of God. A closed fist cannot receive a gift.

Guard your heart against what is not of God and every false way. Deuteronomy 6 tells us to love the Lord thy God with all our hearts, soul and might. Do the opposite of fear. Have faith to believe the impossible. Believe better is possible. A mustard seed of faith is all you need to move a mountain (see Matthew 17:20).

23

SHIFT FROM FEAR TO FIGHT!

Running…I ran from my problems by literally picking up one foot after another and running. I would not acknowledge that there was a problem. I knew there was a problem, but it was like crossing the street and pretending the car coming at you at full speed was not really there. I knew trouble was coming; I could see it before it got there, but I would not make the necessary adjustments to confront the issues at hand.

Once, or twice – okay, really, more than three times – I had my hair done, braided, styled or weaved, whatever I felt like doing. On one occasion, I'd had my hair weaved, and it looked okay. Although, my head was starting to hurt, I just assumed it would go away. The lady asked me if I liked it, and I said yes. By the next morning, my scalp was swollen, and my eyes had slanted upwards because my hair was so tight! I called the lady who did my hair, and she told me to take some aspirin. I did, but there was no relief! The pain was unbearable! I could not take out the braids at that time, because I had to sing with the praise and worship team at church the next morning.

There are well meaning people at the house of worship. They love you, and they support you. Most don't want to hurt your feelings. However, what they may be really saying is this:

"We don't want to tell you how bad your hair looks; so, we are not going to say anything at all. Instead, we are going to stare at you as if there is something wrong and hold back the laughter as best as we can."

Okay, no one said this out loud, but I could tell something was wrong. I am not from the Orient, and neither is my Mother, however, on this day, you wouldn't have known who my Mother was!

As I stepped up to the platform, I know people were looking at me strange. I sang as best as I could, and tried to forget the instant face lift on my face and my swollen scalp.

Fortunately, after church was over, I took off for home to release my scalp from the bondage of this so-called beauty. Only by God's grace, did I not lose my hair! After the pressure of the vice grip of death was released from my head, I could breathe a sigh of relief.

Now, I was not kidding when I said this happened a few times. On another occasion, my hair was braided so tight, it gave me a headache. I called to confront the braider, and she had the audacity to get mad at me! Wow! I am grateful that I still have hair!

Herein lies the challenge: I should have told the truth up front. I should have been honest and said, "My hair is too tight. Can you fix this?"

However, that is not what came out of my mouth. I thought if I said something she might get mad at me.

Like my Pastor says, "So what?" So, what if they get mad at you; there is only one of you. People will treat you the way you think of yourself. If you think of yourself as dumb, then guess what – that is exactly how they will treat you. If you think of yourself as ugly, then that is how they will treat you. You have to contend for who you really are in Christ Jesus.

The Word of God says: "I can do all things through Christ who strengthens me (Philippians 4:13)

You are fearfully and wonderfully made. You are the apple of your Father's eye! You must learn how to fight for what rightfully belongs to you. In this case, it is your identity, your peace of mind and your right to be who you really are. Let me tell you something; you are not a door mat, dirt floor or ratty rug! You are someone very special, but you must recognize that for yourself.

To know who you are, you have to recognize you are a treasure. Look in the mirror and say, "I am someone special." Repeat it again and again until you believe it. But it is going to take more than just looking in the mirror and speaking statements of affirmations. You are going to have to confront the thing that is causing you to back down. You will have to contend with this thing, even after you have won numerous victories, because it lies in wait, waiting for you to let your guard down; so, it can pounce on you once again.

Seven more come in, if you do not fill it with the Word of God. Tag Him in, and ask Him to help you and show you how to win in life!

I started with the Word of God. Here is the funny thing: whatever I was dealing with, I would go to church on Sunday or Wednesday, and guess what? My Pastor would be talking about what I was going through and how to get through it – not stay in it or make a home of it or lay down in it, but how to go through the problem.

I intended to get totally free; so, whatever he told me to do, guess what – I did it. I knew I needed help.

In the past, whenever I had a problem, I would run to my friends, instead of turning to God. I would turn to people seeking the answers I needed. When I decided to turn to God and His Word for what I needed, I found scriptures that genuinely spoke to me. I wrote down the words on 3x5 index cards and read them and spoke them to myself. Change was what I needed and wanted. Those days of being treated like Cinderella were over.

Now, Faith says believe you receive and you shall have. So, I believed I was not scared. Like Joshua 1:8 says, "Be strong and courageous."

Overnight, I did not become the superhero I am today. (I'm smiling at that one.). It took patience, determination and a strong will.

Do you think people will just stop treating you like you are nothing when they see you? No, of course not, not right off the bat. That's because they have no idea of who you are and what you are becoming until you open your mouth and take ACTION on what you believe.

I believe, according to 2 Timothy 1:7, that God has not given me a spirit of fear, but of power, love and a sound mind. For this reason, I did not start any fights, but there were many occasions where I was confronted in terms of who I was.

You see, the devil comes to steal your identity, kill your dreams, and destroy every good thing within you. He will attempt to use anyone or anything to break your focus on being a woman, man, girl, or boy who is not afraid.

I was tired of being bullied, lied on, deceived, and tricked. I was tired of the fiery darts that kept hitting me day in and day out, and the ugly monster of fear had reared its ugly head one time too many.

Praise stills the hand of the enemy, according to Psalm 8:2. I played that card too! I was in the choir at church, and all those songs were in my spirit. I sang my heart out. Speaking the Word gave me a sense of empowerment, and I began to accept the difference that was growing within me. I held my head higher and stuck my little chest out.

Walking with confidence caused people to take another look. People knew there was something different about me. Still, I had yet to learn how to talk to people when telling them NO!

I don't know how long it took, but I'd become a new person. No longer was I a frightened little girl. By opening my mouth, I allowed conversations to come that would bring hope to many.

After I'd gained strength and courage, I had another hair braiding experience during which I did not like the way the lady did it. So, I asked her to redo my hair. She became upset, because she had to go out of her way to take care of it. Yes, I had to change my schedule, as well as she, but am I not worth it? I am!

You also must know when to pick your battles. I'm still on the hair kick. I'd gone to get my hair done by a recommended hair dresser who had her own shop and was doing quite well. We talked and talked, and when I looked in the mirror, my hair was gorgeous! I left the salon, and something in me said, "Check the back of your hair." I did, and a chunk of my hair was gone! It had been cut!

Ok, I will back up a few steps... I'd just left the hairdresser, and she had failed to mention she had "accidently," cut my hair. Angry is not the word I wanted to use at that moment. When I discovered the missing hair, I did not mention it to her, because I knew that I would not be the person who had previously sat in her chair. I would have flipped out! I did not want my anger to cause me to sin. Letting that go was worth it.

Meanwhile, I ended up finding a new hair dresser who had to cut my hair to even it out. It turned out quite nice, despite her having to cut a considerable amount. But you know what? It would eventually grow back. Can you imagine the outcome if I had gone back to the hairdresser who had cut my hair? Even though I was a praying, praising and worshiping woman, I knew that old man in me did not want to lie down and die! And giving to anger at that moment would have caused me to sin.

Did this fiasco cause me to end my relationship with God? No, of course not. Forgiveness is a vital part of your tool box.

24

PUT ON THE WHOLE ARMOR OF GOD

"Finally, my brethren be strong in the Lord and in the power of His might. Put on the whole armor of God that you may be able to stand against the wiles of the devil. For we do not wrestle against flesh and blood, but against principalities, against powers, against the rulers of the darkness of this age, against spiritual hosts of wickedness in the heavenly places.

Therefore, take up the whole armor of God that you may be able to withstand in the evil day, and having done all, to stand. Stand therefore, having girded your waist with truth, having put on the breastplate of righteousness, and having shod your feet with the preparation of the gospel of peace; above all, taking the shield of faith with which you will be able to quench all the fiery darts of the wicked one. And take the helmet of salvation, and the sword of the Spirit, which is the word of God; praying always with all prayer and supplication in the Spirit, being watchful to this end with all perseverance and supplication for all the saints" (Ephesians 6:10-18).

Gear up for battle, and stand and face the enemy that tries to push you back into mediocrity, darkness, fear, bitterness, and hate! Stand with the Lord who sustains you and declare to the heavens:

I will not bow down to the enemy of my soul!

I will stand and fight till the battle is won.

I am created for greatness!

The breastplate you wear is designed to protect your most vital parts. The helmet of salvation, protects your head, because Jesus suffered mental anguish; so, you do not have to, and because you too can be saved by grace. Your loins are girded with the belt of truth, for the truth of the living Word shall set you free. Your feet wear the shoes of peace, for you pursue peace with all men. With the sword of the Spirit lifted high, you declare to the heavens the living Word of God. You are a warrior, fighting the good fight of faith. Know this! Walk in this! Become one with the warrior within!

"COME TO ME ALL YOU WHO LABOR AND ARE HEAVY LADEN, AND I WILL GIVE YOU REST. TAKE MY YOKE UPON YOU AND LEARN FROM ME, FOR I AM GENTLE AND LOWLY IN HEART, AND YOU WILL FIND REST FOR YOUR SOULS. FOR MY YOKE IS EASY AND MY BURDEN IS LIGHT," - JESUS.

25

SHIFT FROM FEAR TO FAITH – RESTING

Rest – to be in a place of full confidence, that is to trust the Lord with everything you are. Give it all to Him, and move in faith, believing without seeing, knowing that all is well.

In this world, you will have turmoil. You will have trials and tribulations. You have not been promised an easy life. However, you are encouraged to trust someone bigger and better than anything you may encounter. Even though you may not have all the answers to all things, what you have need of will be provided to you. You can rest in the arms of the Lord.

One morning, not too long ago, I awoke with a thought. One thought of peace, joy and love – I was focused on Jesus. One pure thought caused an encounter I pray to never forget and has caused me to seek that moment again and again.

"Casting all your cares upon Him, because he cares

for you" (1 Peter 5:7) My heart and my thoughts connected to one sole purpose, and that was to find Jesus. So, guess what I did? I went looking for Him. I knew He had to be somewhere. He'd promised He would never leave me nor forsake me, and therefore He had to be right there!

I opened a book about Jesus, the Messiah, and began to read about His teachings. After I did that, I kept thinking about Him – the name of Jesus, who He was, and that I really needed to find Him.

There were no other thoughts in my head nor in my heart except to "find" him. I can say it was a pure and earnest search for Jesus. I was grateful in my heart, and I kept looking.

I know this may sound comical, but I actually looked under my bed. I was looking for a book about Jesus. I love to read, and there are many books in my house.

The desire to be with Him began to build, and get stronger. I knew I had to get ready for work that day, but I kept searching for Him. Thinking of Him placed me in a different place in my mind and heart; I don't know how to explain this simple joy of looking for Him, but it was refreshing.

I found another book about Jesus, and I read a little of that one and put it down. I did my daily devotional; then I got ready for work.

On my drive to work, I still thought of Jesus, the feeling was still with me. Suddenly, it seemed as if everything melted away. Time literally slowed down. Nothing mattered – not the cold nor the dark, my job, bills that needed to be paid – at that moment I realized only Jesus mattered. In that space and time, I'd found that sweet, delicate, delightful place in Him. His manifested presence was with me!

I was not striving, trying to make something happen. I didn't push or press. I just searched for Jesus with all my heart, and in some way, it was in the waiting I was found. As His presence flooded my vehicle, I was overcome with joy! I smiled from ear to ear, all the while wishing I could stay in this place, to hold on to this moment in time is such a delicate matter.

"He will keep you in perfect peace whose mind is stayed on Him" (Isaiah 26:3).

I felt the joy He has for me! No matter what I'd done, I was forgiven and loved beyond human comprehension. I also knew He was pleased with me. Working to get noticed was the work of the flesh. I didn't have to be prettier, smarter or more disciplined. I only had to be me. I didn't have to pray harder, believe more, or work up more faith to be loved by Him.

In that space, in that moment, I knew He loved me just the way I was, and He accepted me – faults and all! I laughed out loud at this knowledge and at my new understanding of His way. His ways are higher than my ways; His thoughts are not my thoughts, (see Isaiah 55:9).

Total peace surrounded me and carried me on a

cloud of indescribable delight! I felt no fear and no doubt that He would ever leave me or forsake me. I knew! I knew He would take care of everything! He would keep His promise. All I had to do was think on Him.

I encourage you not to ask for anything, just take the time to think on Jesus. Think of His goodness and what He has done for us. Let gratitude be the light in your heart and praise be upon your lips. Seek His presence and soak in His presence. Leave your "wish" list to the side, and just come before Him and wait for Him.

"Let us lay aside every weight and the sin which so easily ensnares us…" (Hebrews 12:1).

Truly and earnestly desire only Him. Let nothing hinder you from gaining Him.

When He calls, listen. Ask, Seek and Knock. Jesus is the answer you are seeking. Rest in His presence. What does that look like? It looks likes trust.

No matter what difficulty you may face, know that He is with you to guide you through. If you decide to stay in that place, He promises He will never leave you nor forsake you. To rest is to let go of your way of doing things and cast all your cares upon Him, for He truly cares for you.

Find a place to dream, to meditate on the Word of God. See the pictures come alive! Place yourself in your dream, and see yourself filled with love and peace. See yourself receiving the answers you have sought for so long. See yourself resting like never before. See yourself helping others, even those who are going through trying times.

Imagine what it feels like to be filled with complete

joy. The smile upon your face is gigantic! Let go of yourself, and fall into the embrace of the Lord. Feel yourself falling and being caught by the One you trust, and you will know he is for you. Know you are loved greatly and adored. Know in your heart, that no matter what you have done, He still loves you. Rest, be at peace and Only Believe...

26

SCRIPTURES*
(From the New King James Version Bible.)

"Death and Life are in the power of the tongue, and those who love it will eat the fruit thereof and bear the consequences of their words." **Proverbs 18:21**

"If you have been snared with the words of your lips, if you have been trapped by the speech of your mouth; so, do this my son and deliver yourself. For you have come into the hand of your friend: Go and humble yourself; plead with your friend." **Proverbs 6:2, 3**

"This is the remarkable degree of confidence we have as believers are entitled to have before Him: that if we ask anything according to His will, that is consistent with His plan and Purpose, He hears us. And if we know, for a fact, as indeed we do, that He hears and listens to us in whatever we ask, we, also, know with settled and absolute knowledge, that we have granted to us the requests which we have asked from Him." **1 John 5:14, 15**

"I will call heaven and earth as witnesses against you today, that I have set before you life and death, the blessing and the curse; therefore, you shall choose life in order that you and your descendants may live." **Deuteronomy 30:19**

"I assure you and most solemnly say to you, whoever says to this mountain' be lifted up and thrown into the sea!' and does not doubt in his heart, in God's unlimited power, but believes that what he says is going to take place, it will be done for him in accordance with God's will. Therefore, I say to you whatsoever things you ask when you pray, believe that you receive them, and you WILL HAVE THEM!" **Mark 11:23-24**

"This book of the law shall not depart out of your mouth, but you shall meditate, read and think on it, day and night; so that you may be careful to do everything in accordance with all that is written in it; for then you will make your way prosperous and then you will have good success." **Joshua 1:8**

"Then the Lord said unto me, you have seen well, for I AM, (actively) watching over MY WORD to fulfill it." **Jeremiah 1:12**

"I will bow down (in worship), towards your Holy temple and give thanks to Your name for Your lovingkindness and Your truth; for You have magnified Your word together with Your NAME." **Psalm 138:2**

"My son, pay attention to my words, and be willing to learn; open your ears to my sayings. Do not let them escape from your sight; keep them in the center of your heart. For they are life to those who find them, and healing and health to all their flesh." **Proverbs 4:20-22**

"I can do all things through Christ who strengthens and empowers me to fulfill His purpose—I am self-sufficient in Christ's sufficiency; I am ready for anything and equal to anything through Him who infuses me with inner strength and confident peace. AND my God will liberally supply your every need according to His riches and glory IN Christ Jesus." **Philippians 4:13, 19**

"For by Him all things were created in heaven and on earth, things visible and invisible whether thrones or dominions or rulers or authorities; all things were created and exist through Him that is by His activity, and for HIM." **Colossians 1:16**

"The thief comes only to steal, kill and destroy! BUT I HAVE come that they may have life, and have life more abundantly. I AM the GOOD SHEPARD. The good Shepard gives His life for His sheep." John 10:10, 11

"Worthy are You, our Lord and God, to receive the glory and the honor and the power; for You created all things, and because of Your will they exist, and were created and brought into being." **Revelation 4:11**

"I am convinced and confident of this very thing, that He who has begun a good work in you will, continue to, perfect and complete it until the day of Christ Jesus, (the time of His return)." **Philippians 1:6**

"Let us seize and hold tightly the confession of our hope without wavering for He who promised is reliable and trustworthy and faithful, (to His Word)." **Hebrews 10:23**

"For WITH God nothing (is or ever), shall be impossible." **Luke 1:37**

"Blessed, (fortunate, prosperous and favored by God), is the man who does not walk in the counsel of the wicked, (following their advice and example), nor stand in the path of sinners, nor sit (down to rest), in the seat of scoffers, (ridiculers). But his delight is in the law of the Lord, and on His law does he meditate day and night. And he shall live like a tree firmly planted, (and fed), by streams of (living), water, which yields its fruit in its season; its leaf does not wither; and whatever he does, he prospers (and comes to maturity)." **Psalm 1:1-3**

"Jesus replied to him, it is written; man shall not live by bread alone but by every word of God." **Luke 4:4**

"For with every heart a person believes, in Christ as Savior, resulting in his justification, that is being made righteous—being freed of the guilt of sin and made acceptable to (God); and with the mouth he acknowledges and confesses (his faith openly). Resulting in and confirming his salvation." **Romans 10:10**

"Yet in all these things we are more than conquerors and gain an overwhelming victory through Him who loved us much that He died for us." **Romans 8:37**

"And do not be conformed to this world but be ye transformed by the renewing of your mind. Take your focus and place it on God and see, and become who you are truly called to be IN Christ Jesus. So that you may prove what the will of God is, that which is good and acceptable and perfect in His plan and Purpose for you." **Romans 12:2**

"He personally carried our sins in His body on the cross, willingly offering Himself on it, as an altar of sacrifice, so that we might die to sin, becoming immune from the penalty and power of sin, and live for righteousness; for by His wounds you (who believe), have been healed." **1 Peter 2:24**

"Give and it shall be given unto you pressed down, shaken together and running over will be put into your bosom. For the same measure that you use, it will be measured back to you. Bring all the tithes into the storehouse, so that there may be food in My house, and test me now herewith sayeth the Lord of Hosts, if I will not open for you the windows of heaven and pour out for you a blessing that you will not have room enough to receive it." **Malachi 3:10**

"He has borne our griefs, and He has carried our sorrows and pains; yet we assumed that He was stricken, smitten by God and afflicted. But He was wounded for my transgressions; He was bruised for my iniquities; the chastisement for my peace was upon Him, and by His stripes I am healed." **Isaiah 53:4, 5**

"And all your spiritual sons will be disciples of the Lord, and great will be the well-being of your sons. You will be firmly established in righteousness: You will be far from even the thought of oppression, for you will not fear, and from the terror for it will not come near you. If anyone fiercely attacks you it will not be from Me. Whoever attacks you will fall because of you. No weapon formed against you will prosper, (succeed). And every tongue that rises against you in judgment you will condemn. This peace, righteousness, security and triumph over opposition, is the heritage of the servants of the Lord. And this vindication from Me, says the Lord." **Isaiah 54:13-15, 17**

"Christ purchased our freedom and redeemed us from the curse of the Law and its condemnation by becoming a curse for us—for it is written: cursed is everyone that hangs on a tree—in order that in Christ Jesus the blessing of Abraham might also come to the Gentiles; so that we would all receive the realization of the promise of the Holy Spirit through faith. And if you belong to Christ, if you are in Him, then you are Abraham's descendants and spiritual heirs according to God's promise." **Galatians 3:13-14, 29**

"For God did not give us a spirit of fear, but of power, love and a sound mind. He has given us a spirit of power love and of sound judgment and personal discipline, abilities that result in a calm, well-balanced mind and self-control." **2 Timothy 1:7**

"Peace I leave with you; My perfect peace I give to you; not as the world gives do I give to you. Do not let your heart be troubled, nor let it be afraid. Let My perfect peace keep you calm in every circumstance and give you courage and strength for every challenge." **John 14:27**

"I sought the Lord, on the authority of His word, and He answered me and delivered me from all my fears." **Psalm 34:4**

"…and to give relief to you who are so distressed and to us as well, when the Lord Jesus is revealed from heaven with His mighty angels in a flame of fire." **2 Thessalonians 1:7**

"We are destroying sophisticated arguments and every exalted and proud thing that sets itself up against the true knowledge of God. And we are taking every thought captive to the obedience of Christ." **2 Cor. 10**

"He sent His Word and healed them all and rescued them from their destruction." **Psalm 107:20**

"Therefore, let us with privilege, approach the throne of grace, with confidence and without fear; so that we may receive mercy, for our failures and find His amazing grace to help in the time of need, an appropriate blessing coming just at the right moment." **Hebrews 4:16**

"And do not be conformed to this world, but be ye transformed by the renewing of your mind; so that you may prove what the will of God is, that which is good and acceptable and perfect, in His plan and purpose for you." **Romans 12:2**

"For I know the thoughts I think towards you, says the Lord, plans of peace and well-being and not for disaster to give you a future and a hope." **Jeremiah 29:11**

"Call unto Me, and I WILL answer you and show you great and mighty things you do not know." **Jeremiah 33:3**

"Delight yourself in the Lord, and He will give you the desires and petitions of your heart." **Psalm 37:4**

"He who dwells in the secret place of the Most High shall abide under the shadow of the Almighty. I will say of the Lord, "He is my refuge and my fortress; My God, in Him I will trust.' "Surely He shall deliver you from the snare of the fowler and from the perilous pestilence. He shall cover you with His feathers, and under His wings you shall take refuge; His truth shall be your shield and buckler. You shall not be afraid of the terror by night, nor of the arrow that flies by day, nor of the pestilence that walks in darkness, nor of the destruction that lays waste at noonday. A thousand may fall at your side, and ten thousand at your right hand; but it shall not come near you. Only with your eyes shall you look, and see the reward of the wicked. "Because you have made the Lord, who is my refuge, even the Most High, your dwelling place, no evil shall befall you, nor shall any plague come near your dwelling; for He shall give His angels charge over you, to keep you in all your ways. In their hands they shall bear you up, lest you dash your foot against a stone. You shall tread upon the lion and the cobra, the young lion and the serpent you shall trample underfoot. "Because he has set his love upon Me, therefore I will deliver him; I will set him on high, because he has known My name. He shall call upon Me, and I will answer him; I will be with him in trouble; I will deliver him and honor him with long life I will satisfy him, and show him My salvation." **Psalm 91:1-16**

"When you lie down, you will not be afraid; Yes, you will lie down, your sleep will be sweet." **Proverbs 3:24**

DAVINA STALLWORTH

Davina is a woman who experienced and lived in fear, and allowed it to become her closest confidante. Through a journey of faith, she discovered her true identity and is now living in her true calling, to comfort, edify and encourage those who are living in fear themselves.

Davina has been graced with the wisdom of God to speak to those who have been hurt, lost and forgotten; she brings words of comfort to help others find true peace. Through her writings, the heart of God and His unending, unconditional love is revealed to bring hope, comfort and joy to people young and old.

www.ingramcontent.com/pod-product-compliance
Lightning Source LLC
La Vergne TN
LVHW021346080426
835508LV00020B/2129